convergence

Brett Johnson

Published by The Institute Press

The Institute Press, Inc.
4535 W. Sahara Ave.
Suite 100A 576
Las Vegas, NV 89102
www.theinstitutepress.com

Printed in the United States of America

Library of Congress Catalog Number Applied For

table of contents

Lyn Johnson, my wife of 20 years, is a remarkable woman. She has added her own unique thoughts to the content of Convergence— the Funnel for hearing God speak is one example. She has grasped the nettle of integrating our lives and ministry, and she has been a delightful partner in living a life of intentional obedience. The story shared in this book is our joint story. Had she written it, the story would have been more colorful and exciting.

A simple Acknowledgement does not begin to capture the gratitude I feel for the hundreds of hours of conversations I have had with friends about the promise and practice of Convergence. There are those who have challenged me to dig deeper to find out who I am so that I could articulate my story. And there are others who have allowed me to dig a little into their lives as I have explored their stories.

To Iain Muir, Mike McCandless, and David Boyd who sparked me into action.

To Lucile Allen who has been a gift to us as the official Editor of Convergence. To Dr. Charles Self and Dr. Art Wouters who provided extensive guidance and built their own contributions into the content.

To the Time Out committee, especially Dave Dias and Ryon Paton who provided an opportunity to share thoughts on Convergence in 1997 at a Time Out retreat they helped organize for Silicon Valley executives.

To the many people who have been through Convergence seminars in different formats and have provided helpful critique. To those who have passed through our home, drunk tea, visited long, stayed up all night.

I would like to specially acknowledge our colleagues at *The Institute for Innovation, Integration & Impact* who have shaped my thinking and refined the frameworks used in this book. Their ongoing application of the 10-F model to Institute clients has led to fresh understandings. They have been a personal incubator for me as I have struggled through how to live an integrated life.

Thank you

acknowledgements

THE EVENTS BEHIND CONVERGENCE

Iain Muir is a solid Scottish Chartered Accountant turned missionary. With over 30 years of mission experience, he has a worldview as robust as his Scottish brogue. Since we began a friendship in 1981, I have come to value his counsel and quick insights. When visiting me in California some years ago he told me about something he had read or heard on the subject of *convergence*. He referred to the writings of Bobby Clinton[1]. To my chagrin I did not buy the book, but the concept stuck in my mind. For years I have pondered the notion that for some people there comes a time when all the events in their personal history begin to hang together for a greater purpose.

Mike McCandless, a friend turned colleague, sat across from me at a Mexican restaurant in Belmont, California a few years later. "You ought to write a book. I believe in the power of the printed word...You should write a book." That statement caused me to examine my passion. I am not a writer by profession, but I have been sensing for a while that more of my time should be spent writing. I tucked Mike's suggestion in my cogitation box.

David Boyd is an integrated thinker. As Chancellor of the University of the Nations in Kona, Hawaii, he became a friend as a result of the consulting work we have done with the University. As part of a strategy project addressing the question, *What does it*

[1] J. Robert Clinton, *The Making of a Leader*, NavPress, 1988

mean to disciple a nation? We had recommended that the University develop a Center for Integrated Development—a nation in a building. Based on the notion that *networking* could be the organizing model of the future, we suggested that the University of the Nations' mission would be served if students and leaders could see all aspects of society represented in one place. They would then be able to understand how the different parts relate to each other.

As Lyn and I flew home from that week's assignment in Hawaii, we reflected on a major career decision we were facing. Our challenge was not the enormous task of discipling a people group, but the issue of how one holds the competing segments of one's life in healthy tension. Both the University's and our decision revolved around the principles of integration. With the "why not write a book" challenge still brewing in the kitchen of my mind, it seemed God was leading me to make a career change.

TOUGH CHOICES

To backtrack a little, my career began with Price Waterhouse in Cape Town, South Africa, and I went on to spend fourteen years with them. By 1993 I had switched firms and was a partner in the consulting division of KPMG Peat Marwick. After several years in that position, I felt that God was directing me to relinquish my partnership at KPMG Peat Marwick and move to a large systems integrator. At Computer Sciences Corporation (CSC) I had repeated the now familiar pattern of starting ventures from scratch. Having built a thirteen million dollar consulting practice in less than three years, one could safely say things appeared successful. So when I suggested to my superiors that I hand my practice over to a replacement and start on a new venture, they were a little surprised. To some degree, so was I. But it was a response to a divine directive that happened this way.

PROGRESSIVE GUIDANCE

I was driving up Interstate 280 one morning in December 1995 heading for a strategic planning meeting. The idea was to figure out what our office of CSC might do in the future. I was supposed to have spent time over the weekend pondering potential strategies. Now it was Monday morning and I was caught in a tight spot praying the ludicrous: "God, got any good ideas?" Immediately an idea popped into my mind, "Start an institute." So I floated the idea past my colleagues: we should start an Information Technology (I.T.) Transformation Institute. Clients would come to us for consulting and we would be a center of excellence, etc. They liked the idea. Later, however, the marketing director came to me and said, "I like your idea, but I think it might be a little too narrow. How about something linked to value disciplines[2]?" Increase the vision–music to a visionary's ears.

A few weeks later I was driving to work again and felt God ask me three questions.

1. Are you willing to start an institute?
   Yes, Lord.

2. Are you willing to ask the President of CSC Consulting for two months of pro bono consulting as a condition of starting the institute? Some years before a friend had called and said she felt I was to make a Nehemiah-type request to my employers, asking for an amount of time off. This seemed to fit.
   Yes, Lord.

3. And are you willing to trust me for the revenues?
   God had proved himself faithful in this area before. When I had left KPMG I had taken a $75,000 cut in base pay, but I had sensed that God had wanted me to trust him with my finances. Things had worked out well, and I saw my practice revenues grow from two million to ten million in less than two years.
   So I answered again, *Yes, Lord.*

Pursuing the formation of some sort of institute became a matter of obedience, not a matter of good career planning. I settled on the notion of a Customer Value Institute that would focus on the creation of customer value, an upside, rather than the slicing and dicing often associated with reengineering corporations.[3]

[2] Treacy and Wiersema, *The Discipline of Market Leaders*, Addison-Wesley Publishing Company, 1994
[3] Michael Hammer, James Champy, *Reengineering the Corporation*, Harperbusiness, May 1994.

Our family was in the midst of this decision when we flew to Hawaii to consult to the University of the Nations. During the return flight Lyn said to me, "You need to pursue the institute idea on your own. If it is successful at CSC, they will demand more and more of your time, and you will have little time left to serve missions leaders." Time had become a challenge for us. We had started e-Quip (formerly Professionals for Christ) in 1992 when I had about 30 "personal days" each year. At CSC I was down to 15 days of vacation a year. Fitting in the pro bono consulting was becoming a challenge. Soon the decision was made. I would leave CSC and we would start The Institute on our own. More on this later.

BACK TO THE BOOK

David Boyd was back in town for one of his many visits. I shared Mike McCandless' book idea with him. "If you had to write a book, what would you write about?" he asked. "I guess I would write about how one integrates one's business life with one's calling."

For many years I have watched people struggle with the desire to "do missions," whatever that means, and balance their work and home lives. Most of it stays in the realm of good intentions. I became convinced that the issue was not motive, but failure to recognize and respond to God's leading.

In my own life I have always been bi-vocational. For many years Lyn and I were unpaid youth pastors, Sunday School teachers/superintendents, and, later, pastors for about five years—all while holding a demanding job at Price Waterhouse, and consulting a few missions organizations. Well-intentioned people pressured me to "go full-time" when I was already working 40 to 50 hours a week pastoring a church and working simultaneously in the business world. (I was about as full-time as it gets!) There was also the internal pull to do missions "full time" or just devote all of my efforts to my career. Yet doing solely one or the other—business, local church leadership or missions—would have been the easy way out. I am convinced that God wanted us to learn to live with the tension and figure out ways to integrate the different spheres of life.

Convergence was born out of our own story. It comes from our personal struggle to learn to manage the tensions resulting from:
• The compelling cord of Career
• The stretched strands of Community
• The thin threads of Creativity and
• The silver strands of Call

Convergence has been woven out of our attempts to do what God seemed to be telling us at a given point in time. Looking back, we can see some threads running through our lives. Our hope is to share them with you so that you, too, can see an integrated tapestry woven in your life.

1.

To say that life is pressured is to say that Everest is a hill. To say that key areas of our lives are increasingly in tension is a similar understatement. We have been bludgeoned by a barrage of time-squeezers that leave even the most astute time managers beaten down. Complicating things is the fact that many of us gain our primary sense of identity from what we do, or our Career. Any sense of a greater purpose for our lives—our Call—is often suffocated by our Career, which has wrapped its tentacles around who we are.

> A U.S. Senate Subcommittee in 1965 predicted that by 1985 the average American would work a 22-hour-a-week workweek and would be able to retire by age 38. Instead, since 1973 leisure time for the average American has decreased 37% and the average workweek increased from 41 to 47 hours!

True Creativity should not take away from our Call. But Call can be obscured by entertainment and endless imaginings. There's the fantasy that says, "One day I'm going to quit my job and become a _____ (fill in the blank)." Dreams and the pursuit of pleasure can sidetrack us from Convergence. We undoubtedly have subscribed to the work hard/play hard philosophy. Americans spend 11-12% of their income on leisure (as opposed to 1.5% on charitable giving.) So the tension between Career and Call is probably overshadowed by the work/pleasure cycle. Work, play, work, play.

While we have seen trends of Cashing Out[4] and Cashing In[5], for many on the treadmill there just doesn't seem to be enough time or encouragement to stop and ask whether the work hard/play hard game is the only one in town.

If you have a family, you'll more likely feel tension between Career and Community. In our definition your community includes family, friends and affinity groups such as church and clubs. For most people, once this battle has begun there is hardly enough strength to clean the weapons for next week's recurrence of the fight, let alone ammunition to open another battle front.

If you are part of the burgeoning single-and-thirty-something set, the pulls and pushes will be centered around your identity. Who am I? How do I define myself sans children, et al? How do I create legitimate goals so that I am not consumed by the avoidance of aloneness? Can I achieve Convergence without a life mate? Without the disciplines of dependents shaping my calendar, how do I focus on the right things?

Every now and then I run into someone who has a notion to do some great feat of faith, but their family doesn't want to fall in line behind the vision. When one cuts to the chase, the family members do not oppose the Call, but they legitimately fear the cost to their Community. The absence of an integrated framework leaves them insecure, suspicious that they will be neglected while the Call is being pursued. This Call/Community tension is common.

WE ARE EASILY POLARIZED

The net result of these conflicts is that we have become a polarized people. The points of disconnect between the major areas of our life seem to outweigh the strands of integration. One good choice—the decision to follow Jesus—does not guarantee that the rest of our decisions will be as sound. As long as we have breath in us, we will have the ability to do our own thing. Some of our choices will be of little consequence; others will nudge us onto a path that meanders towards mediocrity. Few people seem

---

[4] Lys Marigold and Faith Popcorn, *Clicking,* Harperbusiness, January 1998

[5] A recent *Newsweek* article spoke about the trend of yuppies who cannot afford to cash out taking lesser pay ing jobs at organizations whose cause they are willing to support.

to possess enough grace and grit to respond to God's apparently absurd initiatives over a long enough period of time to enjoy Convergence. The alternatives are just too appealing: successful career, nice cars, kids in "right" schools, looking good, big corporate/church title, fitness fanaticism, job security. Many travel these highways yet miss the off-ramps that could lead to Convergence. In our attempt to keep it all together, we lose it. Big time.

And yet there is an encouraging new wave of people asking how we can connect life's strands in a way that meets our deepest needs while still providing for the basics of everyday life.

THE RATE OF CHANGE, THE INCREASE OF ALTERNATIVES— THE AVALANCHE OF DISTRACTIONS

Breakthroughs in information sciences are creating tremendous opportunities, not just in the digital revolution, on the worldwide web, or for full-blown nerds. The implications are coming to a grocery store near you.

- **Consumerism:** The number of different items (SKU's or Stock Keeping Units) in food stored in America increased from 10,000 in 1986 to 35,000 in 1996. Every day, catalogues flood into homes around the world offering stuff, stuff, and more stuff.

- **Biology:** Thanks to the field of genomics—the blend of biology and information—130,000 new strands of corn were created in 1997.

- **Technology:** The explosion of information technology and information is re-raising the 1980's issue of the difference between data and information. Until filtering and smart technologies advance, individuals are left to sift through the rubble on their own.

- **Globalization:** It used to be a buzzword, but fueled by the boundary-less internet, we are now starting to see quick intercontinental ripples begun in Asia, Silicon Valley or Washington DC ponds. Organizations are learning to create global ripples but lack the skills to manage them, if they are indeed manageable.

- **Confluence of information, communications and entertainment:** This leaves individuals, particularly younger people, needing discernment to figure out what's real and what is hype in the game of life.

- **Economics:** The 1997/98 Asia economic crisis quickly became a global crisis (see Globalization.) The economic rules for the 21st Century have yet to be written. The medium of exchange is even uncertain—will it be information; intellectual property; food?

- **Career opportunity/uncertainty:** Depending on whether "every silver lining has a cloud," or vice versa, there will be a surge of new opportunities for the "information haves" and a less bright future for the "information have-nots." Deciding how to chart your future when the job you will do may not have been invented yet causes career anxiety.

Information, alternatives, distractions. Life's highway has evolved from a straight road with periodic, predictable markers to one lined with flashing neon signs, exits, on ramps, and cheap motels. If that were not enough, the inside of the vehicle has surround sound, a 6-stack CD changer, telephones, intelligent guidance systems and talking control panels. We should be better guided. Yet we are desperately in need of a True North. How do we sift through the mire of muchness? We need to know our Call. We need life skills that give us a shot at Convergence.

HOPE IS FLEETING

No sooner have pundits declared world peace than the headlines read Global Recession. Technology breakthroughs promise quality of life while the millennial bug or virus de jour eats away at our security. Unimaginable wealth from stock appreciation is followed by rumors of crashes. If we look to things around us, we will be hopeless. If we look within us, we will be no better off. "Hope deferred makes the heart sick," says the proverb. But if we listen to God's voice through the babble of the world, we will have hope.

WE ARE RUNNING LOW ON MARGIN

There is another reason why we need Convergence. Our segregation of Career, Community, Creativity and Call often manifests itself in the erosion of what Dr. Richard Swensen calls "margin".[6] Margin is the shoulder of the road. Rather than having a safe shoulder between danger and ourselves, we often find our vehicles scraping the median. We look worse for the wear.

It is difficult to tackle matters of Convergence when we have no slack in our rope. Before we can meaningfully develop strategies for Convergence, we need to assess the degree of margin in our lives.

Much work has been done to divide the human person into different categories. Mind, body, soul, spirit—these are typical components dating back to ancient times. In Luke 2:52 we find a one-verse synopsis of 18 years of Jesus' life:

> "And Jesus grew in wisdom and stature, and in favor with God and men."

Many of us would like to have that etched on our teenage years. And whole teachings have been founded on this verse to promote the balanced Christian life: Wisdom (mental), stature (physical), favor with God (spiritual) and favor with man (social). For years I tried to plan my days on this basis. But this notion of "balance" was not enough.

THE 10-F MODEL

I needed a greater granularity for my planning to be more meaningful. So in the last ten years we developed the 10-F model (covered at the end of this chapter) to help analyze margin, assess contentment, and make planning more pragmatic.

I have a friend who has more talent than the average basketball team, twice as many kids as the average American, a mortgage to die for, a passionate desire to be something significant for God, and the day-to-day

---

[6] Richard A. Swensen, *Margin*, NavPress, March 1995

realities of keeping a larger-than-average family glued together. One morning as I snaked along the San Andreas Fault the phone rang in my car. I pulled up to the nearest restaurant and was soon joined by Kent.

As usual, Kent had more pots on his stove than burners to put them on. Sensing a leading to give up a secure management position and create a new role for himself in his company, he would be walking out on a thin limb which seemed supported only by mist. While exciting for Kent, there were a few complications. This mist-walk might require more time at work. He felt he didn't spend enough time there; his wife felt he spent too much. Second, he sensed that the job transition was part of a longer-term solution that would give him an opportunity to pursue his life dreams; but his dreams were his wife's nightmares that threatened family time and food on the table. As we had breakfast, I asked Kent a series of questions that were designed to give him the tools he needed to find his own future.

The following exercise takes you through those same questions.

- Circle the numbers that best indicate your contentment in each area. The objective is not to get perfect scores, but to get a clear perspective of yourlife.
- "5" means you are very content and probably have lots of margin; you are experiencing plenty of grace in this area.
- "3" means you feel somewhat stretched, but you know what to do to remedy things. You are feeling some pressure in this area, but you are not without grace.
- "1" means you feel squeezed, perhaps strung out, and you are running low on contentment. Even if you know what to do to fix things, you are currently out of margin.

10-F ASSESSMENT FORM[7,8]

Circle the number of the comment which best applies

Fun	1	2	3	4	5
Fulfillment at Work	1	2	3	4	5
Function in Society	1	2	3	4	5
Fresh Thinking	1	2	3	4	5
Finances	1	2	3	4	5
Fitness	1	2	3	4	5
Friendships	1	2	3	4	5
Feelings	1	2	3	4	5
Faith	1	2	3	4	5
Family	1	2	3	4	5

[7] Dr. Charles Self, See article on *The Biblical underpinnings of the 10-F Model* © I⁴ International, 1999
[8] Dr. Art Wouters, See article on *The Psychological underpinnings of the 10-F Model* © I⁴ International, 1999. Both articles can be found under Thought Pieces at www.convergencebook.com

WHAT HAS MARGIN TO DO WITH CONVERGENCE?

Expecting to wake up one day and discover that we have arrived at Convergence is hugely unrealistic. We need to give ourselves—and God— the margin needed to make things happen. Some years ago I met a Jewish believer who had worked a steady job as a schoolteacher in New York. As a new believer he realized that if he stayed in his job and failed to risk, there would be little opportunity for God to bless him. So he took a job for less pay, worked for a tough boss, and became a millionaire. I am not a "name it and claim it" proponent, but his advice to me has stuck: Put yourself in a position where God can bless you. Make yourself available to God—practically. Absence of margin works against this principle. What is true for Finances is valid for the other 9-Fs.

A rabbi told a story that went like this: A religious man stood in the syn- agogue and asked God to help him win the lottery. That week he won nothing. The next week he was back in the synagogue asking a bit more fervently. Silence from God and no big win. By the third week he was prostrate before the Ark, begging God to help him win the lottery. Just then a voice came from the Ark. "Look, would you mind meeting me half-way. At least buy a ticket!" We've all been like that man. We want the joy when God does great things in and through us, but we are so busy getting ready in the locker room that we never get in the game. To win, you have to be in the game. To get in the game, you have to make the time and space to play. That's why margin is important to Convergence.

THE ROOT AND THE FRUIT

If we are short on margin, how did it happen? How did we become a peo- ple with our Career, Call, Community and Creativity at war with each other? The root of our fragmentation is in our thinking. Unless we address the root of dichotomized thinking, we will reap the bad fruit of fragmentation (and the associated loss of margin) in our lives.

2.

Sculptor Korczak Ziolkowski was invited by Sioux Chief Standing Bear to carve a memorial to the Indian people. A television documentary covered the progress of the carving of Crazy Horse into a huge granite face of the Yellowstone Mountains. Clearly this work was going to exceed the life span of the sculptor. He has since died and the sculpture is far from complete. Yet his children continue the work. Current estimates are that it will be completed without Federal funding by the year 2050. The sculpture of the warrior astride a stallion will be 563 feet tall. That's eight feet higher than the Washington Monument and nine times as high as the faces of the four American presidents carved in Mount Rushmore, just a few miles north of Crazy Horse.

Why go to this effort? In an interview the late Korczak Ziolkowski stated:

> "When your life is over, the world will ask you only one question: Did you do what you were supposed to do?"

When Michelangelo was painting the Sistine Chapel he was told, "This may cost you your life!" His reply? "What else is life for?"

These two artists from different eras had a similar view of their work. The question to you is, "What is your life work?" It's a tough one to answer.

THESIS

We often hear "God loves you and has a plan for your life." We also see two extremes in figuring out just what that plan is. On one hand, Short-term Teri faces every grocery purchasing decision as though her spiritual life depended on it; on the other hand, Nebulous Nick doesn't believe he can ever know God's plan. Convergence counters both near-sightedness and fatalism.

Convergence also helps us wear spectacles that have two different lenses: with one we see the big picture—the horizons—and delight in God's big design. Through the second we see the minutia of today—drudgery and all—and worship God energetically in it, and through it.

The basic thesis of Convergence is this; following God's leading reduces the tension between the major areas of life. And following God's leading is easier if you recognize and understand the road signs along the way. The road signs take the form of seven major seasons.[9] These are covered in subsequent chapters.

Convergence is about completeness, about closure, about contentment. Some people do great things, but have no contentment. Others know that they have done what they came to do.

Paul said: I have fought the good fight, I have finished the race.	→	Michelangelo had no assurance of his spiritual prospects in the after life.
John Wesley founded a movement that far outlasted his years.	→	His counterpart, Whitfield, built in his own words "a rope of sand." He did amazing things (much in conjunction with Wesley) but was not too content with the life results.
Jesus prayed "I have brought you glory on earth by completing the work you gave me to do."[10]	→	"Don't let it end like this. Tell them I said something." — Pancho Villa's last words

---

[9] Clinton's book, *The Making of a Leader*, tracks the typical phases in the life of those called to pastoral or ministerial work. The different phases are sequential and well explained. Having developed these materials before I was able to eventually track down his book (using Amazon.com) we had taken a road that was somewhat different from the sequential route. Our view has more to do with seasons than sequence.

[10] John 17:4

CONVERGENCE: DEFINITION

Roget's Thesaurus offers an explanation of Convergence that is short and sweet: "to direct towards a common center."

We put a spin on the definition of Convergence that sees it in three categories:

The Process of Convergence: The coming together of those important deposits built into your life over the past 40 or so years, resulting in the discovery and walking out of your life Call.

The Activities of Convergence: Your cooperation in understanding, preparing for, and walking into your Creator's life purposes for you.

The End of Convergence: The discovery of those threads which, when woven together at a particular juncture in your life, cause you to say, "Yes! This is me; this is what my life is for."

Convergence is not necessarily about setting out to do great things. Convergence comes through setting one's face towards a walk of obedience that is carried to completion. In this book we hope to direct four separated areas of life—Career, Community, Creativity, and Call—towards a common center.

THE COMPONENTS OF CONVERGENCE

An absence of Convergence is often the result of the fragmentation of four key worlds within our individual worlds. We call them the four Cs:

Career, Creativity, Community, and Call

The tapestry of Convergence is a weaving of the interrelationships of these areas. To discover Convergence one must understand Integration.

My own background includes the field of "systems integration". The company I worked for was known as a "systems integrator." This embodies the notion of getting different "things" to work together efficiently to achieve some business purpose. Organizations need systems integrators because of the complexity of aligning people, processes, software, hardware, communications networks and other technologies to work together, not just to be functional, but to deliver a specified result.

The concept of Integration reaches well beyond the realm of systems integration. It's a centuries-old life framework that has been a key organizing principal of philosophers and greengrocers alike.

In the March 29, 1999 issue of *Newsweek* an article by Kenneth L. Woodward entitled *2000 Years of Jesus* points out that Jesus Christ changed many things. He caused an "inversion of values" with his focus on the poor, the "discovering of the individual" and the "redefining of male and female." Jesus was not about "business as usual." He made a radical difference in the world. And the first thing that Woodward notes is that Jesus introduced a "new conception of God." Quoting theologian David Tracy of the Chicago Divinity School, he says:

> Now, as in modern physics, we are coming to see that all of reality is interrelated. The doctrine of the Trinity says that even the divine reality in all its incomprehensible mystery is intrinsically relational.

Integration is inherent in the nature of God. He is perfect, and that perfection includes the perfect interrelationship of the Father, Son and Holy Spirit.

Yet this past century has emphasized specialization and the never-ending quest to sharpen our focus, be more precise. The explosion in knowledge has forced professionals in many fields to filter out everything that detracts from a narrow specialty. Add to this the increased competition in the macro and micro work environment and the demands this places on one's career, and we have the ingredients for a fracturing of the once interrelated areas of life. Work, family, church and relaxation strain and tear. When these areas become disconnected, we have "disintegration."

In the business world, Michael Hammer and Jim Champy were among the first to realize that this was inefficient and, therefore, costing companies lots of money. Their writings caused a wave of "business reengineering" across corporate America. At the center of reengineering was the integration of processes across business functions. The results were often spectacular, but not always spectacularly good. The human toll was often enormous. Unfortunately, the executors of reengineering projects often lacked a comprehensive philosophical framework that considered integrating other areas into this massive process change.

On a larger scale, the tight fiscal policies of the International Monetary Fund (IMF) in Asia are said by some to have caused the Asian Economic Flu in part because they ignored the cultural, political and people issues in those nations. Optimization is not the same as Integration. Optimizing one area can yield good short-term results for individuals and organizations. Sustained impact comes, however, from integration.

Integration emanates from the understanding that God is for the whole of life. 2 Corinthians 5:16-20 makes an amazing statement:

> So from now on we regard no one from a worldly point of view. Though we once regarded Christ in this way, we do so no longer. Therefore, if anyone is in Christ, he is a new creation; the old has gone, the new has come! All this is from God, who reconciled us to himself through Christ and gave us the ministry of reconciliation: that God was reconciling[11] the world to himself in Christ, not counting men's sins against them. And he has committed to us the message of reconciliation. We are therefore Christ's ambassadors, as though God were making his appeal through us. We implore you on Christ's behalf: Be reconciled to God.

In the past my focus on this text had been on the individual. Verse 20 clearly says, "Be reconciled to God." My problem was that I had equated that with my personal "day of salvation" (although I cannot tell you exactly when that was) and assumed that reconciliation had to do with a mostly one-time mending of an estranged relationship. But I now see more than that in verse 19 which says, "God was... reconciling the world to himself." Two things have changed in my thinking:

[11] (My Teachers Commentary) A ministry of reconciliation (2 Cor. 5:11-21). To understand this passage, we must realize first that Paul was not talking about evangelism when he spoke of his "ministry of reconciliation" (v. 18). "Reconciliation" literally means to "bring into harmony." When we set our watch by the electric clock in the kitchen, we are "reconciling" our watch to the clock. We change the one so that it keeps time set by the standard of the other. This is what Paul wanted for the Corinthians; to bring their lives into harmony with the pattern set by God.

- Reconciliation is an ongoing process of bringing into alignment anything in my life that is out of alignment with Truth. It is a process of integrating the many aspects of my life by overcoming, through Christ, the sin that has caused separation.

- The world is broader than individual relationships. "All things are from God" and reconciliation—or integration—includes the alignment of all elements of life.

People are desperately hungry for integration. They cannot always put a name to it, but they want the whole of their lives to have meaning, seven days a week.

Howard grew up in Northern Ireland, became a believer at about eight, went to university, and pursued a career in banking. By the time I met him he had been a partner in a global investment banking firm, had orchestrated multi-billion dollar financial deals, lived all over Asia.

But there was another side to Howard and his wife Liz. They had grown up in a church tradition that valued what others would call "lay ministry." Howard enjoyed teaching the Bible. He had been an elder for many years, providing effective leadership to teams of elders in various local churches. He enjoyed ministry.

I received his resume from a mutual friend and when Howard and I chatted on the telephone he was looking to create a work situation that would allow him to divide the year between work and ministry. My response was simple: "Come and visit me, and I will show you that you really desire to do "ministry" 100% of the time, whether for missionary organizations or for-profit corporations."

The language of the Church allowed Howard to express his plans only in terms of "full-time vs. part-time" and "work vs. ministry." But it was easy to sense that what Howard really meant was that he loved the business world and he loved serving missions and local churches. He wanted to minister to business leaders in their offices, and to pastors in their pulpits. He wanted to apply all of his gifts—whether honed in business, with his family or in the local church—to all of his life. And he didn't want a salary to be the differentiating factor between work and ministry. And his heart really sang out the theme that God is for the whole of life, not 10% here and 30% there and 60% somewhere else.

A framework of Convergence helps the Howards of the world make the right decisions.

THE FUTURE IS ALMOST PRESENT

When the rate of change is very, very fast, as it is today, the future is almost now. When society is reinventing itself every three to five years (according to some), the person with the six-year forecast is a futurist. Today someone predicts a technological or societal breakthrough at some future date, tomorrow you read about it in the newspaper. So why become a trend-spotter?

> "My people are destroyed for lack of knowledge."[12]

> "The sons of this age are shrewder and more prudent and wiser
> in relation to their own generation than are the sons of light."[13]

Following the trends is not necessarily a path to Convergence. Sometimes God asks us to walk in the opposite direction of a series of major trends. Nonetheless, it is generally helpful to understand the major trends so that we can better understand what God is up to (or sometimes up against), and how he might be leading us. By the time you read this, some of what follows may be out of date. But if you pick up the habit of trend spotting, you will have learned a skill that will serve you well as you seek to make wise decisions.

CAREER TRENDS

Almost everything is changing on the career front. The job market has undergone radical shifts in the 1990s. The old career rules no longer apply. What used to be respectable stability is now lack of marketability. It's not yet clear whether the new trends are better, but it is clear that they

[12] Hosea 4:6
[13] Luke 16:8 (Amplified Bible)

are very different. Reengineering has both helped and ravaged companies. The number of people employed by Fortune 500 companies has dropped from around 16 million in 1990 to 11 million in 1995. The fundamental shift to an information-based economy is in full swing. The Internet in particular has exceeded all growth projections and will continue to be a yeast that alters the shape of many industries. It is an enabling technology that is allowing huge changes to take place in the way that we see and do work. Many of the jobs that will provide our income in the 21st century do not even exist yet. Let's take a look at some of the major trends affecting the "C" of Career.

Trend	Implication for Convergence
Globalization: People from around the world can compete for your job, and most of them for less money.	You have to continuously re-tool so that you maintain sought after skills. And, there are new opportunities for the brave "across the ponds." Further, you will need to discover Convergence in a global context.
Family friendly policies: More and more organizations want to appear to be family friendly. Few employees feel the freedom to take advantage of these policies.	People recognize when there is a difference between stated policies and unspoken values. Don't believe everything in the policy manual. If you want integration between Career (work) and Community (including your family), get ready to make tough choices. They may be good choices, but they won't always be easy.
Work as Community: Some corporations are attempting to create a home-like atmosphere for work. Mrs. Grossman's Paper Company and AutoDesk allow dogs at work; some companies have on-site day care; workers decorate their factories any way they please. With job security no longer an option, smart employers are turning in other directions to make work seem more like a community.	The softening of the hard edges between home and work will allow the fortunate few to overcome the dichotomy between work and earning money. But ferns and fluffy pets won't be enough if the fundamental values of the organization are not aligned with the soft side of the company.

Trend	Implication for Convergence
The shifting location of education: Education originally began in the home. Religious institutions then assumed the education role, with a later shift to public schools.	In recent years corporations have taken on the role of educator. With the availability of home-accessible information via the Internet, will this fuel the shift of education back to the home? And with the growing information empowerment of The Millennial Generation (Y), will they self-manage more of their education? This emboldened self-management of education may be a pre-cursor to the self-management of Careers.
Cashing out: Many have tasted success, not liked the aftertaste, and cashed in their stock options.	People are starting to look for alternate careers earlier in life. The new millionaires are younger, and less likely to know who they are. Career success can outstrip character development, leaving more questions than answers.
Cashing in: Those without the means to completely leave the workforce still have the wherewithal to cash in their stock options and pension plans and move to lower paying jobs. And many are doing just this.	Some people are content to take lesser paying positions that enable them to do meaningful work, often going to work for non-profits at a fraction of their former salaries.
Home-based businesses: There has been a tremendous growth in home-based businesses in recent years. About 25,000 new businesses start in homes in the U.S. each month; 80% of these are successful in the first two years (compared to the old statistic of 80% of new businesses failing in the first five years.) 60% of these new ventures are run by women.	The large corporations are no longer the only respectable career option. Gone are the tape-recorded background office noises, the muffler on the dog, and the long-winded explanations of why the client can't actually come to your office (a.k.a. Armando's Mailbox Service.)
"In the future, the distinction between work and spare time will wither away because, increasingly, the demands we put on our leisure time will be the same ones we put on our work. We are approaching a fully integrated life."	People will seek jobs with greater meaning, and spend more time working at such jobs. But the distinctions between such work and play will blur. Working holidays will increase, people will find it harder to discern true priorities, and without a stable values base, people will be more sold-out than ever to their Career.

One should not be too quick to predict that a blurring of Career and Community is a good thing. Some corporations will be quick to jump on this trend for their own benefit. "Corporate America harbors a dirty secret," says *Fortune* magazine. "People in Human Resources know it. So do a lot of CEOs, although they don't dare discuss it. Families are no longer a big plus in a corporation; they are a problem."[14]

Regardless of whether corporations have holistic approaches to family and work, the rap on Career is that it still gets the bulk of our energy. This is not a bad thing. Scripture has much to say about working hard and honestly. The question should not be whether we love our work, but whether it has become our primary point of significance. For many, the worship of work indicates that we are still finding our identity in our work, and not in our God.

Work—*occupacio*—is good. Call—*vocation*—is better. Convergence is about making the choices that maximize the harmony between these concepts.

I sat opposite a successful businessman at lunch one day. As a fairly young millionaire he had reached a stage in his career that Bob Buford might call "halftime."[15] Except that he wasn't taking a rest between periods, he was in meltdown mode. After 20+ years of career success he was struggling to face the prospect of coming out of the locker room for the second half. Others saw him as successful, but he knew that the money trail did not lead to a settled identity. When we hurtle down the hollow hallways of our jobs desperately seeking for identity, our pace becomes more and more frantic for fear that we will be overrun by the deafening echo of our own empty steps.

The career trends could lead to two distinct possibilities. One is meaningful work without the sacrifice of the other areas of life. The other is a redefinition of work as being the place "where it all happens" and family as a source of utility-type services such as food, laundry and sleep. "For many people today, home has primarily become the place where a lot of routine work has to get done—duties that won't wait: doing the laundry, cooking dinner and taking care of the kids. Home has become a treadmill. At work, there is a higher level of service; people have time to talk and have fun."[16]

---

[14] Betsy Morris, "Is your family wrecking your career?" *Fortune*, March 17, 1997
[15] Bob Buford, Terry Whalin *Halftime: Changing Your Game Plan from Success to Significance* (April 1997) Zondervan Publishing House
[16] Rolf Jensen, *The Dream Society* (1999) McGraw-Hill

There are career trends that point to a more family-friendly world, but we must be warned that the benefits are not automatic. If we carry any seeds of fragmentation out of the locker room, then instead of a more fruitful second half, we will reap the same crop we had going into half time. The dangers of dichotomy will be amplified in the future.

Which leads us to a discussion of Community.

COMMUNITY

Community looks a little different for each of us. Traditional definitions of peer, support and accountability groups are up for grabs. The jury is out on electronic communities, the impact of technology on relationships—good and bad—and the role of traditional nuclei of community. Regardless of how one defines community, it is often at odds with Career. Somehow Community takes second place to our love affair with doing. The net result is that we are increasingly isolated. The larger the city, the quicker the pace, the greater the isolation. Without Community we suffer.

Newsweek magazine reported radically different health effects of simply being in relationship with supportive people.[17] Women who answered the question "Do you feel isolated?" with a *Yes* were three-and-a-half times more likely to die of breast, ovarian or uterine cancer over a 17-year period. "Does your wife show you her love?" According to *Newsweek,* men who answered *No* suffered 50% more angina over a five-year period than men who said *Yes.* And heart patients who felt the least loved had 50% more arterial damage than those who felt the most loved. Unmarried heart patients who did not have a confidant were three times more likely to die within five years. "Do you live alone?" Those heart attack survivors who said *Yes* were more than twice as likely to die within a year.

Independence is a two-edged sword. In the U.S. it is prized right along with "life, liberty and the pursuit of happiness." In fact, many probably confuse the *pursuit of happiness* with *independence,* and *independence* with *leaving one's social and family structures as quickly as possible.* Said another way, American parents may be far too quick to push their

[17] Newsweek, March 16 1998, "Is love the best drug?"

children out of the nest. Friends once told us that others would view them as suspect if they said that their 17-year-old daughter was going to attend a community college and stay at home during that period. "What about the Big 10, the Ivy League... all will be lost!" We prematurely dismantle the social infrastructure of our children, and then wonder why they struggle to create community of their own.

Have you noticed that many of the successful TV sitcoms are simply about people in community? *Seinfeld, Mad About You, Friends, Fresh Prince of Bel Air, Growing Pains...* The newer series involve community at work. Inwardly we seem to long for community. Outwardly it is often quicker and easier to turn on the TV and meet our pseudo-friends who care for and get mad at each other, rather than take the time to build our own community. Yet week after week millions of people turn on the tube because of a deep longing for community. (Note also that much of the Community depicted on TV nowadays is based around work: Career and Community are converging.)

So what are some of the major trends impacting Community?

Trend	Implication for Convergence
Speed and superficiality replace longevity and depth: Much of our world is becoming transient: our jobs, hometowns, technology, etc. This has a spillover effect on relationships.	We readily accept as normal the vacuous black hole that was once community. We have to rekindle hope in Community because we find our Call in serving others, or in the context of community.
Roll-your-own community: We used to accept the menu of primary community-providing groups, such as a local church. More and more people are defining their own small groups and not paying much attention to the formal prescriptions of organizations.	Given that this trend is starting with teenagers, there could be an increased likelihood that we fail to grow up with a 'balanced diet' of community. Whether for its big-picture oversight or its pedestrian predictability, if community erodes we may be more susceptible to disintegration. Rampant personal consumerism could exact a high price.

Trend	Implication for Convergence
Rediscovery of roots: Globalization makes us rootless... or does it make us hanker for our roots? With the lack of certainty on life's busy streets, many are retracing the path back home. Not to live there, but certainly to know where *there* is.	Understanding your personal DNA can help you figure out your Call. This is good. On the other hand, a preoccupation with preserving the family heritage (especially if you think you come "from good stock" or if you were born with a healthy trust endowment) can lead to simply repeating negative family patterns instead of blazing new trails. Wisdom, please.
Resurgence of spirituality: The public admission of adherence to religion of all kinds is evident everywhere.	This popularization of spirituality can both open the path to Convergence, and create the illusion of "any path will get you there." The theories of "the journey is the way" can sidetrack many from pressing in to find true Convergence. By the same token, more public awareness of man's need for a spiritual foundation creates a forum for an inner dialogue about the whys and wherefores of our lives.
Integration of family: There is a rising tide of "family first." I commonly meet with business people who are open about commitments to being home over the hour of doom—5.30 to 6.30 p.m.—and reluctant to make appointments at times when they should be with their families.	We must overcome the destructive assumption that Call will take away from family. If we drag this deficiency from the world of Career to the other areas of life, we will be no less satisfied than we were before. The banner of "sacrificing for Jesus" is more likely wallpaper over our disintegrated thinking than God's call to isolated living. On the positive side, people are jealous of precious time with their families. The deliberate integration of family into one's life paves the way to Convergence.

Today we need Community more than ever. But lifestyles and demographic changes are challenging the traditional assumptions about where we find Community. For believers, the traditional place of community has been the local church. Is this changing? A universal answer at this point would be premature. Early signs, however, indicate that people are exercising a greater degree of self-management in forming or joining groups that meet their needs. This extends to areas of fellowship traditionally organized by a single local church. This Chinese menu approach goes something like this: I will attend Sunday services at church A; I like the evening worship at church B, and the fellowship groups (home churches, Bible studies, care groups) of neither. So a group of us from various churches will get together when it suits us. This lack of local church community cohesion has down sides for everyone concerned, but reflect the tolerance, independence and self-management of our times.

The "going to work/having spare time" separation that came about in the Industrial Age is beginning to reverse itself. There is a window of opportunity for the Church to become a community of relevance as society is once again in the throes of redefining itself.

The bottom line is this: it will be hard to get to Convergence without Community. We discover ourselves in the context of community. Others shine a light on our gifts and grim realities. People inspire us, refine us, and multiply our efforts innumerably. No Community, no Convergence.

CREATIVITY

Before we go on, a clarification on what we mean by Creativity might be helpful.

"In the beginning..." God is way ahead of us in the creativity department. At first glance his general modus operandi was to create something out of nothing. He simply stated it, and things came into being. Now if you don't subscribe to creation as articulated in the early chapters of Genesis, this book will probably do nothing to change your views. I have to point out, however, that Creativity is key to Convergence. And the creative process that we employ today is not so different from God's creative process. In fact, it derives from him and therefore looks like his process.

Before we explore this further, notice that the creativity of which we speak has little to do with leisure. It is essential to relax. The leisure industry has grown in leaps and bounds. We spend a huge percentage of our disposable income on travel and entertainment. In short, we work hard, and we play hard. At least that's the way we justify our wild fluctuations and adrenaline dependencies. But is it good for us, and if not, is there another way?

Creativity is not the twice-a-year pleasure rampage. The starve/binge approach to "creativity" is not healthy. Second, if we are talking about leisure and being built up, there is another way: entering a rest, Sabbath. With our grocery stores open 24 hours a day, malls and gas stations open on Sundays, and the ripple effects of "separation of church and state" spilling into commercial life, it is hard to maintain the sanctity of a holy day. (This is not a grand religious statement, on my part, or a hill to die on; it is an observation of reality.) Strict observance of the Sabbath as a day when no work can take place was maybe once a bondage. Today it appears to be much less of a bondage than the enslavement that people have to work—followers of Jesus included. We are also enslaved to communications (How many of you have forgotten to turn your cell phone or pager off when you're in church? Who takes their cell phone on a bike ride?), and sports (Sunday games for kids are not uncommon) and many others things that keep our engines running on high revs. It's hard to be creative when you are worn out.

When looking at Creativity I am including what we do with a paintbrush and palette, a pottery wheel or software code. These and many other areas are essential to our well being, but I am probably not the person most qualified to talk about them. There is great pleasure in reflecting God's creativity in the everyday, particularly in doing what the scripture calls "practicing hospitality."

Beyond this, I want to unpack the joys of getting alongside God and finding out what he is up to, then climbing on his bandwagon. This is where we go back full circle to the process of creation: seeing something where others see nothing, articulating it, and causing it to come into being.

> "God is the god who gives life to the dead and calls things that are not as though they are."[18]

---

[18] Romans 4:17

But I am not a visionary! you say? So what? God called you out of one thing to something else. You at least need to get a picture of yourself being wrapped around the form of Jesus. That involves some change. Then the wonderful privilege of being called to be co-workers of Jesus Christ means that we all have the responsibility of figuring out what he is up to, and how we can serve what he is building. You may not be wired to be a trailblazer or a pioneer. You may be a settler who comes behind to establish the infrastructure and law and order that creates a place where others can live. But this too requires vision. It involves creativity. It involves faith.

So the Creativity of which I speak is, in part, a creative faith. And we need to integrate this creativity into our homes, our work and the pursuit of our call.

"Now faith comes by hearing, and hearing by the word of God."[19]

He speaks and things come into being—in creation and in you and me.

Trend	Implication for Convergence
Innovation comes in small packages: One of the great strengths of the U.S. economy is its unstoppable innovation. Yet the bulk of innovation in the U.S. comes from companies with fewer than 19 employees.	We separately need creativity and innovation in our work and personal lives. While creativity might historically have been for recreation, now we need things that build us up incorporated into the fabric of our work lives.
What we might do tomorrow doesn't exist today: Many of the 21st Century jobs don't exist today. Rapid changes in technology will make obsolete much of what we considered to be "bedrock of society" jobs.	We need to pay closer attention to the creative side of our lives. Our ability to adapt, reinvent ourselves and nimbly follow God's initiative will be key to our success.
The quest for creativity in work, and meaning in play. "In the Dream Society, free time will occasionally be difficult to distinguish from work and —above all—it will be imbued with emotional content..."[20]	On the down side, our children will see us as constantly working. ("That wasn't a vacation... you were working.") On the plus side, there will be a vastly expanded number of opportunities to find or create jobs that embrace our creativity.

[19] Romans 10:17 The word here is *rhema*, not *logos*. It is the spoken word of God, not the written word of God. Reading the Bible raises our hope level; God speaking something to us gives us faith, the faith to create. This once again reinforces the importance of the season where we learn to hear God.

[20] Rolf Jensen, *The Dream Society* (1999) McGraw-Hill

Before leaving the subject of creativity, some will read into Creativity an advocacy for "the contemplative life." Contemplation is good, but when it leads to isolation and the rending of everyday life to a so-called secluded life, we open ourselves to distortion. In the writings of the early Church there was "the perfect life" and the "permitted life."[21] An over-emphasis on "secluded being" as distinct from "everyday being" is as dangerous as the elevation of *doing* above *being*.

CALL

Every believer has a call upon his or her life.

 That's easy to say, but when someone asks, "How do I discover the call of God for my life?" it is not so easy to answer. Like personality, gifts and character, the call on our lives has two different but equal facets: it is the same for everyone, and it is different for everyone.

What is the same for everyone? The Westminster Confession states that the chief purpose of man is to glorify God and to enjoy him forever. This is universal. We are made in the image of God, and we understand ourselves and our context as we get to know him better. This is the fabric of every believer's tapestry.

But call seems to go beyond this broad purpose. It takes on a flavor of something specific to you and to me. So the flip side to our common purpose is that this God is infinitely creative. He has decided that each of us is best off when we reflect the unique facet of his character that shines only through us.

The ways in which people "received a call" are many and varied. In the old days we seemed to hear more about "receiving a call" than we do today. And when we heard about it the context was generally someone explaining how they were "called" to "full-time Christian ministry" or to a particular "tongue, tribe or nation." If it was "spiritual" it was a call, or if the location was remote and preferably African-sounding, so much the better.

---

[21] Os Guinness, *The Call*, Word Publishing, 1998 - page 32

The rest of us didn't talk about Call that much. How often have you heard someone say, "I was called to IBM." "That's nothing. I was called to General Electric."

And I was called to Price Waterhouse and San Francisco. Seriously. When I was completing my undergraduate work at the University of Cape Town, the Big 8 accounting firms did their spiel on campus. I don't recall seeing any of them. I simply prayed and felt that God would have me go to Price Waterhouse. My friends lined up interviews with many companies. I went to one. During the interview the Staff Partner, Anthony Coombe, asked where else I was interviewing. "Nowhere else. I believe I am to work here." He graciously extended me a job offer.

I then spent 14 years with Price Waterhouse before being called on to my next skills-building situation at KPMG Peat Marwick. Being called to a place meant that I understood well that "promotion comes from the Lord." It freed me from the pressures of needing to carve my own career (politically speaking—in the creative sense, I did carve my own career as both firms provided wonderful opportunities to trail-blaze in new areas), and also left me the freedom to leave when I felt God wanted me to move on.

The move from KPMG to Computer Sciences Corporation was another such move. Logically speaking, it was a little crazy. Less money, more work, less prestige—a potential CLM (career limiting move.) But through prayer and much confirmation from my bible readings, I felt I had learned what I was to learn at KPMG. It was time to move on for other reasons too. I wanted to travel less. My daughter was entering her pre-teen years, and I would not have the opportunity to repeat them. And it turned out that there were wonderful aspects to the culture, skills and quality of people at CSC that complemented what I had learned at Price Waterhouse and KPMG. The main point is that I felt called to move. Now is a call to First Baptist Church or XYZ Missionary Movement any more real or valid than a call to business? Not in my book.

Now, as much as I felt led to work in each of those organizations for different seasons, they were not in and of themselves my Call. My call has to do with being a living example of the integration of business and missions in a way that creates a bridge for others to find a way to walk out their vocation without necessarily abandoning their occupation.

Trend	Implication for Convergence
Working for a higher purpose: It's been said that if we can't enjoy our work, we should at least enjoy the reason for our working. But today people want both: they want meaningful, enjoyable work.	Employers are going to have to (a) create more enjoyable work environments and, more importantly, (b) craft a vision for their organizations that supercedes the processes and tasks of the organization.
A new understanding of occupation vs. vocation: "I fish therefore I am." "I work therefore I am." We've all seen the T-shirts. But the momentum nowadays is with the growing group who say "I am therefore I choose what I do."	Consider how much of what you do at work is consistent with how God wired you. One measure of this is your grace barometer: does your work build you up or let you down? How much Call is there in your career?
Dissatisfaction with the temporary: Research shows that the satisfaction of a new purchase (such as a car) fades after just 21 days. We are increasingly dissatisfied with temporal things.	Watch out for the Convergence concealers. When a pursuit of things keeps us perpetually riding the 21 day curve, we will be less sensitive to the whisper that is Call.

When I planned to leave CSC and start The Institute I met with the man who was then president of the consulting division. After a few sentences of explanation, he interrupted my dialogue to state that he would: "go to his grave believing that I had made a mistake leaving CSC." Less than an hour later he remarked, "We want you to stay, but if you have this higher Call on your life..." I hadn't used the word Call. I did not lay out the alternatives: God's way or your way. But he saw it clearly. How did he recognize the call on my life? Like some other things, Call can be hard to explain, but you know it when you see it.

WE NEED A CALL, AND WE NEED A CONTEXT

Without a frame of reference outside ourselves, we will implode on ourselves. Without an external voice calling us beyond ourselves, we will lack the realistic vision to be other than who we are at the moment. God calls us to be and do not because we are able, but because the Call itself will require us to stretch and go. Call is not just a validation of who we are, it is an appeal to grow to the next level.

The second thing to note is that our call comes in a context. Each of us is placed in a context, or frame of reference, or sphere of influence. For some it is the Arts, for some the Sciences, for some Education, and for others Government. For many it is Business, yet they hanker for the other side of the fence where "real ministers" have "real Calls." Come to terms with your context, then minister 100% to God and others in it.

OUR CALL MUST COME FROM GOD

The word *call* can be used loosely by those inside and outside the Church. Despite the many sources of inspiration, there are numerous reasons why our call must come from God:
• Only he can create a vision beyond us and provide the grace and power to ratchet us beyond superficiality and slothfulness
• He provides a goal—it is him, his likeness
• He provides a source—it is his being
• He provides a reason—it is his love
• He provides a path—it is his Son, Jesus
• He provides a means—it is his Spirit.

No one, nothing—not ourselves or this world—can ever begin to make us this offer.

"From him and through and to him are all things."[22]

Convergence is not the result of a decision you make once. It is not the result of a single planning session. It is more often the fruit of an integrated mind, the harvest of lots of little decisions. Some of your decisions have pushed you in the direction of Convergence; others have side-tracked you. The older you get, the lengthier those side-roads seem to be.

Convergence is an all-too-rare phenomenon. Sadly, I have met many chronologically gifted people who have done many things, traveled to

[22] Romans 11:33-36

many places, seen lots of "ministry," but have yet to experience the fullness of God's purposes for them. There is no formula that predicts or explains when individuals will experience Convergence. God works differently with each of us.

Finding the wisdom spoken of in the book of Proverbs has some parallels to experiencing Convergence. If we learn to listen, we will hear it cry out. If we learn to read its road signs, we will begin to see the path it is taking us on. If we are aware of its principles, it has a way of drawing us towards it. This, I suppose, is part of the mystery. It happens in God's time and in his way, but we can understand it, accept it and even hasten it by God's grace.

> "If you accept my words
> and store up my commands within you,
> turning your ear to wisdom
> and applying your heart to understanding,
> and if you call out for insight
> and cry aloud for understanding,
> and if you look for it as for silver
> and search for it as for hidden treasure,
> then you will understand the fear of the Lord
> and find the knowledge of God."[23]

Words, commands, wisdom, understanding, insight, hidden treasure, fear of the Lord... knowledge of God. This is our goal.

---

[23] Proverbs 2:1-5

• Take a moment to consider the four Cs listed below and indicate the approximate percentage of total energy that you expend on each category. The total should add up to 100%

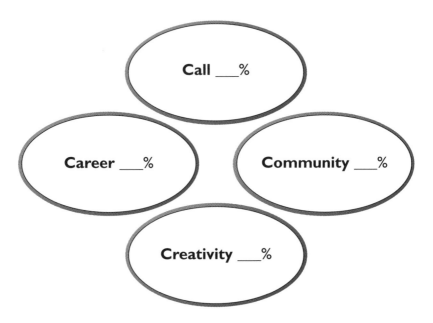

Call ___%

Career ___%

Community ___%

Creativity ___%

• To the extent that these 4-Cs overlap in your life, what percentage of your efforts lies at the overlaps of the 4-Cs?

• What is your context? If you had to draw a box around all 4-Cs and label it, what would that label be?

3.

CONVERGENCE IS NOT BALANCE

I'm not sure that balance is a biblical concept. While it was helpful to me as a new believer to compartmentalize my life and make plans for each area, I'm not sure that the goal of balance was altogether trustworthy. Obedience sometimes demands that we be unbalanced. When I meet people today I often ask, "What's your passion?" I seldom ask "Are you balanced?" For well-rounded people the question is a nonissue; for unbalanced people...what's the point in asking?

CONVERGENCE IS NOT A FORMULA

Second, Convergence is not designed to be formulaic or prescriptive. This is no Three-Easy-Steps-to-Life program. Simple answers to life are often just that.

During Jesus' three brief years of public function, many adept religious people scurried left and right trying to box him in. And yet the Jesus of the gospels carefully escaped the predictive packaging of the establishment. Jesus was clear, yet mystical. He was fresh, yet established in eternity. He was single-minded, yet vigilantly avoided the narrow-minded arguments with which his followers and opponents sought to tether him.

We recognize the dangers of 4-Cs and 10-Fs and other tools in this book. So we ask that you not look to these ideas as a way *out,* but as a way *to.* (Should you find yourself becoming formulaic in your thinking, stop to rediscover where Jesus is taking you.)

Convergence is about the mystical. It's about fine-tuning our senses to the mysteries of an unlimited Creator. It's about discovery—discovering yourself, learning to know and tell your story, gaining a perspective of how that story fits into the grand sweep of your Father's story.

To gain this perspective and to better participate in what God is initiating, it helps to have pens and a palette. It's useful to create markers and milestones that illuminate what has happened in our lives. So don't think of Convergence as the day planner for the next century, but as the toolbox of the mystical. We all need to sharpen our tools to understand, not just God's plan for eternity, but what the Bible calls his ways, his paths, his dealings. We need a forensic kit so we can rediscover the fingerprints of our Creator on the seemingly random pieces of our short lives.

One of my favorite verses comes from Proverbs 25.

> "It is the glory of God to conceal a matter;
> To search out a matter is the glory of kings."

Come be a king for a day.

In a letter to Chuck Colson, Father Tom Weinandy wrote:

> The true theologian or church body wishes to know ever more clearly the mysteries of the faith so that...we know better what the mystery is, not that we comprehend the mystery and so deprive it of its mystery. ...with the clarity [of doctrinal purity] comes more mystery - more awe, more reverence.[24]

Our goal is to bring clarity to the mystery—not to reduce the mystical to a formula—and cause us to be more in awe, more reverent, more fearful of the living God.

CONVERGENCE DOES NOT NECESSARILY EQUATE TO SIGNIFICANCE

Each of us likes to feel special; most of us would rather be a "somebody" than a "nobody." We often express this as a need to feel significant or to have significance. In and of itself, this is not bad. But the quest for sig-

---

[24] Charles Colson, *The Body,* Word Publishing, page 98

nificance can be dangerous. In his book, *Perilous Pursuits,* Joseph M. Stowell opens by saying:

> "We are built for significance. Our problem is not that we search for it, but that we search for it in all the wrong places."[25]

Believers in business are facing an unprecedented opportunity to find significance in all the right places. The Founding Partners of the *Life@Work* magazine, Tom Addington and Stephen Graves, state their belief that "for the past 20 years, *family* has been a front door through which the Gospel has been introduced to Americans." But they see the early decades of the next century belonging to the world of *work.* This would not be the first time God has birthed mission waves out of the business incubator. The stage has been set for business people to have worldwide influence. The reach of companies and their leaders is world-wide in part through enabling technology such as the Internet.

Writings and organizations that spur others on to find meaning in life beyond the sometimes lucrative daily grind have emerged in recent years. Bob Buford's books, *Halftime*[26] and *Game Plan,* have struck a chord particularly with baby boomers and previous generations that are seeking ways in which to move from "success to significance."

We see a new trend emerging. Generation X and the Millennial Generation, perhaps predictably, want the direct route to significance, even if it means trading in success. (Many I speak to want both, but the point here is that they want meaningful work right out of college.)

Convergence, like other writings around this subject, can be prone to a formulaic interpretation. But in Isaiah 55:8 we are cautioned:

> "For my thoughts are not your thoughts,
> neither are your ways my ways," declares the Lord.

Regardless of what stage of life we have reached, if business has a mandate for missions in the next century, we will have to be a people who are finding out what it means to do things God's way. The rest of the Isaiah 55 passage gives us insights into the key to Convergence.

---

[25] Joseph M. Stowell, *Perilous Pursuits,* Moody Press 1994, page 13
[26] Bob Buford, Terry Whalin *Halftime : Changing Your Game Plan from Success to Significance* (April 1997) Zondervan Publishing House

As the heavens are higher than the earth, so are my ways higher than your ways and my thoughts than your thoughts. As the rain and the snow come down from heaven, and do not return to it without watering the earth and making it bud and flourish, so that it yields seed for the sower and bread for the eater, so is my word that goes out from my mouth: It will not return to me empty, but will accomplish what I desire and achieve the purpose for which I sent it.

When sharing the Word of God with people we are often quick to claim as a promise: the Word won't "return void." But sometimes things are spoken into our lives and they do not come to pass. (This can be a good thing if the credibility of the source is dubious.) We need to note, however, that "it will not return to me empty" follows a clear understanding that God does things his way. And his way is not our way. And his thoughts are not our thoughts.

It is also important to note the phrase, "so is my word." In the section on Fearing and Hearing God we elaborate on this truth. Convergence comes as we respond to God's initiative. God's initiative is revealed in what he speaks, and these "words from God" produce the faith to follow God.

"Faith comes by hearing... the word of God."[27]

So Convergence has much more to do with obedience to God's word—written and spoken—than a specific pursuit of significance or any business formula for missions. In fact, in many instances obedience leads to insignificance. If God's leading in your life parallels the life of John the Baptist, Jesus will increase, and you will decrease. If obedience to God's call means significance in the eyes of the world, well and good. But this is the wrong measure. For our significance results from our secure identity in Jesus, and not in the dubious views of success or the accolades of people. Our secure identity leaves us free to serve. And service, among other things, leads to significance. Illusions of significance can rob us of contentment. Likewise, caring too much about what others think of us leads to consternation, not Convergence.

"Do nothing out of selfish ambition or vain conceit, but in humility consider others better than yourselves."[28]

[27] Romans 10:17
[28] Philippians 2:3

Jesus is the best example of a secure person laying aside an easy route to significance in selfless obedience:

Jesus, knowing that the Father had given all things into his hands...
(He was secure in his positional authority)

... and that he had come from God
(He knew his roots and identity)

... and was going to God
(He was very clear on his destination)

...rose from supper and laid aside his garments... and began to wash the disciple's feet.
(He was able to follow a path of service, precisely because he was so secure.)

Our question should not be, "How do I find an outlet for my great gifts and talents?" but "How has God created me to best serve others with my unique collection of talents?"

Now that we have considered what Convergence is not, let's take a look at Convergence in leaders through history.

4.

While still resisting the urge to reduce Convergence to a formula, let's take a closer look at some of the leaders whom we admire in history. It's often easier to figure out what happened in their lives than in our own, and almost always easier to do in retrospect.

Leader	Early life	Skills/Call	Character	Convergence
Joseph	Dreams	Duties	Dungeons	Dynasty
Moses	Selection	40 years in training	40 years in desert	40 years of national leadership
Esther	Exile, training by uncle	Selection as queen	Rejection (for a season)	Rule
David	Duties	Anointing	Desert	Kingship
Daniel	Exile	Training	Lion's den	Governing
Jesus	Suffering, exile	Launch, Divine commissioning	Desert	Ministry
Mary	Promise	Relocation	Mother of Messiah	Place in history
Paul	Training	Call	Desert	Effectiveness

Several things are worth noting about these and many other leaders in the pages of the Bible.

- They all began nowhere, and yet somewhere. Moses floating in the basket on the river Nile, Joseph one of twelve sons, Mary a teenager in the village. Not many of them have noble beginnings, yet somehow we know that God began his work when they were "knit together" in their mothers' wombs.

- For many there is a definite commissioning of some sort—a dream, a choice of a leader, a prophecy, a word of a parent or relative. Sometimes others are more tuned in to our destiny than we are, especially when we are young.

- For most there is a delay between the call or commission, and the fulfillment of that call. This is perhaps the toughest thing for us to handle. We are so accustomed to immediacy. We get so wrapped up in *my* career, *my* plans, *my* timeline, *my* ideas of my life. Yet God is not bound in his thinking about time.

There are not exact answers, but try to estimate the amount of time between God's call/word to these leaders, and their walking it out:

Leader	From	To	Number of Years
Moses	Call to lead	Red sea	
David	Anointing by Samuel	Public coronation	
Jesus	First acknowledgement as Messiah	Public ministry	
Paul	Damascus road	Recorded ministry	

• Later we will provide a more detailed framework for observing the path to Convergence. For the moment, consider three contemporary leaders who seem to have experienced Convergence. What are the major phases they have been through in their lives? How have these phases impacted their ability to contribute?

Leader	1st Phase	2nd Phase	3rd Phase	Convergence

TIMING IS EVERYTHING

We hear it so often that we forget its importance. The world's technology dump is filled with products that hit the market too soon or too late. "I was five years ahead of the times." "We were just three months too late to market." And the now famous snowboarders' lament: "I coulda dun dat first!"

"Timing is everything!" This is not a core biblical truth, but an understanding of timing sure helps and, as followers of Jesus, we often run into trouble because we don't understand it.

In my own life, after getting initial direction, I am learning to ask the second question: When? About how long are we talking about here? Long term, or short term? Way off, or pretty close? Any other clues as to timing? I don't think God objects to these questions.

Don't get me wrong. I am often surprised by God's timing and how his plans and mine are out of sync. But I've found that it doesn't hurt to ask. One of my most valuable lessons in this area came in 1987 when Lyn and I were praying about whether to start Professionals for Christ/e-Quip. In summary, we felt it was right. We were to stay in the U.S. as missionaries to start an organization that would bridge the worlds of business, missions, and local church. In prayer with other leaders, I felt God say that he would give me the blueprints of the new ministry (which he did). As I meditated a while longer, I sensed God say that there would be a five year ramp-up period. So I stashed the ministry blueprints, and quietly enrolled in the University of the Desert. If I hadn't sensed the timing, I would have been frustrated and wasted a lot of people's time. The fact is, for the next four to five years I did not have the "umph" to do anything except wait.

While we may seldom know the exact timing, God takes most people through a series of major seasons, which we will consider in the next section.

5.

KAIROS AND CHRONOS

Technically, I am an African. My father was born on a farm in Sea Point, a suburb of Cape Town, South Africa. While my mother only arrived in the city of Port Elizabeth when she was eight years old, she is an African. She has a South African passport, her formative years were spent in South Africa, and she lives in a small town in South Africa. My four older siblings and I were all born in South Africa, making us Africans too.

Practically, however, no one in my family, with the possible exception of my youngest son, David, is very African, especially when it comes to a concept of *time*.

As a child I was amazed to watch real Africans interact. There is much to mesmerize one in Africa. The gentle rhythm of women-folk walking with a load balanced perfectly on their heads and a child tightly wrapped in a blanket on their backs; the leisurely lilt of their voices; and the fact that a conversation with a pedestrian passing the other way began long before they were shoulder to shoulder, and continued until they were virtually out of earshot. The rhythm of Africa is different. It not driven by *time* as we know it, but by events or seasons.

In the translation of scripture to English we have lost the nuances of *time*. *Chronos* and *kairos* are two distinct words referring to *time* in the Bible. Chronos is the root of chronology and chronometer, the official name of a watch or timepiece. We are driven by time. We have 101 ways to master it, make it go slower, get more out of it, put more into it, get more because of it. We have whole industries devoted to helping us slice and dice the 168 hours we have each week. We measure our worth in time. If we have money, we easily say, "Time is more precious than money," and almost mean it. *Chronos* we know; *chronos* knows us, and controls us.

But cousin *kairos* is a stranger. For *kairos* speaks of time as a season. It is the notion of the rightness of the timing of something that is greater than the calendar or the chronometer. In biblical revelation, *kairos* controls *chronos*.

"In the fullness of time..."[29] At just the right time, the right season. Africans know *kairos;* Westerners know *chronos*. The James Strong Exhaustive Concordance of the Bible defines *kairos* this way:

> "an occasion, i.e., set or proper time; convenient, due season; (due, short, while) time, a while."

My daughter, Fay, is a westerner, depressed by the phenomenon of her 15th birthday because it reminds her of how young she is. Wanting to be older. Anticipating the future, but not content with the season of being 15.

How about you? Are you driven by *chronos,* or sensitive to *kairos?* Where *chronos* is important, do you have it working for you, or against you? (See more on this in Convergence and Young People.) To answer these questions we must first develop a grid for sifting through *kairos* and *chronos*.

---

[29] Galatians 4:4 and Mark 1:14,15

• Take a look at the following scriptures and indicate which seem like *chronos* and *kairos* to you. (A Greek concordance would help.)

Reference	Scripture	Chronos	Kairos
Matthew 2:7	Then Herod called the Magi secretly and found out from them the exact time the star had appeared.		
Matthew 8:29	Have you come to torture us before the appointed time?		
Mark 1:15	The time has come. The kingdom of God is near.		
Mark 10: 30	[No one] will fail to receive a hundred times more in this present age...		
Luke 1:57	When it was time for Elizabeth to have her baby...		
Acts 7:20	At that time Moses was born...		
Romans 5:6	You see, at just the right time, when we were still powerless, Christ died for the ungodly.		
Colossians 4:5	Walk in wisdom toward them that are without, redeeming the time. (KJV)		
Rev. 12:12(b)	He is filled with fury, because he knows that this time is short.		
Rev. 22:10	... because the time is near.		

• How have you thought about time in your past: primarily *chronos,* or *kairos?*

• What are two or three *kairos* moments in your past?

If one view of time were a sub-set of the other, what would it look like?

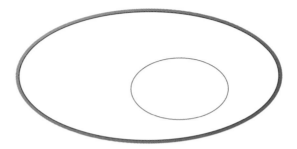

LIFE BEFORE CONVERGENCE

What do people usually go through before they get to Convergence?

This is the question I wrestled with as I lay in the sun on a deck chair in Cancun. (Someone has to do the hard work.) As I spent a good while chatting with God and reflecting on my own life I began to realize that I had passed through seven seasons before reaching the front gates of Convergence. With the background understanding of *kairos,* I was able to discern the major seasons in my life, some of which had run in parallel:

• Faith (and knowing God)
• Fearing and Hearing God
• Discovering Gifts
• Internal Integrity
• Skills Building
• Re-choosing My Spouse
• University of the Desert

I was about to launch my own company. This was something I had considered before, but sensing the season was not ripe, had set it aside. I had often started things in the past; I like to blaze a trail. But with The Institute a looming reality, I had to ask myself some tough questions: Was this just the Forty Year Itch? Hadn't my father left a secure job at about the same age and struggled financially after starting his own businesses? (Or was he really successful despite the economic downscaling he had undergone?) Was I ready? Had I been through adequate preparation?

Part of the answer lay in the Seven Seasons. While I had been through some of the seasons more than once, not one of them was avoided. As I reflected on God's handprints on my life and what had transpired, I accepted that I was on the verge of Convergence, not implosion. The edge still looked a little scary, but Lyn and I had committed years before to live on the edge.[30] Convergence was "not the end, nor the beginning of the end" but just, in Churchill's words, "the end of the beginning." It was both the culmination and the start of our personal story.

Jesus seemed to like stories. He was a master-storyteller, using them skillfully to teach timeless truths. He never wrote a book, but we remember his stories 2000 years later. The Master Storyteller also loves people, and he made each of us unique—a unique part of his story, if you like. Each of us has our own special story of how God is interacting with us and shaping our path.

If each of our stories is unique, it stands to reason that the order in which we experience the Seven Seasons differs from person to person. There is no particular merit to a specific order of things. Unlike the more linear demarcations of career progressions[31], our observation is that *kairos* is no slave to *chronos*. Having said this, there are often two seasons that are bookends to the others: Faith (knowing God) and The University of the Desert.

It is easy to rationalize why Faith may not be the first season, and it is true that in each story the season of coming to know God may come at any time. But, more often than not, it is the season that gets us going down the road to Convergence. At the opposite end of the Seven Seasons stands the University of the Desert. I call it God's Finishing School. Regardless of when this season is experienced, we don't get to Convergence without it.

So, get a handle on your story. Others will benefit as they relate to it in some way. You will benefit as you face the hurdles, past and present, that

---

[30] Recommended reading: Loren Cunningham, *Daring to Live on the Edge*, YWAM Publishing, September 1996

[31] Dr. J Robert Clinton's book, *The Making of a Leader*, covers the sequential stages of development of leaders with a predominant focus on those in "fulltime Christian work." While his use of a sequential model differs from our use of seasons, I recommend his book to those seeking a greater understanding of their leadership development.

keep you from grasping your own story. And, true enough, while your story is unique, it is the same. No matter; it bears telling. (A later chapter provides some tools for telling your story.)

One final thought: as you learn to understand your life story in the context of seven seasons, don't make the mistake of viewing God's involvement in your life as beginning from the day you wrote your name on a card and "made a decision." God made a decision to love and pursue you before this earth was established.[32] While you came to know him at some point in your story—or perhaps you're not sure you know him yet—he has known you longer than that. As you explore your seasons, remember that his fingerprints were on your life long before you decided to follow him.

WHAT SEASON ARE YOU IN?

"Been there, done that."

This is a common 90's phrase...and it bothers me. From the same genre as "Whatever!", it smacks of an unwillingness to be open to what God may have in store. You hear it from people eager to indicate that their resume is complete. The question is not "Have you been there and done that?" but, *What happened to you when you were there and doing whatever "that" happened to be?* After their first tour around the desert, how would God have responded if the people of Israel had said "Been there, done that," when God told them to take another lap?

The seasons in our life are not measured in terms of some heavenly checklist. If you are half like me you'll be trying to mark off all the sights on the Holy Land map as you skim through this book. If we opt for this cursory crash course, we might miss the essence of the Seven Seasons. They are threads woven into the tapestry of our lives as we "lay hold of that for which Christ laid hold of us."[33] Christ is the audience of our tapestry, but he is more than that. He is also the designer, and weaver, and he weaves himself—his lifethreads—into your tapestry and mine.

Remembering that Convergence is not formulaic—we are not trying to "connect the dots" between Seasons—we will begin to explore the Seven Seasons and give you an opportunity to consider where you've been and where you are today. So let's pull back the dust cover from your tapestry and see what God has been doing thus far.

[32] Ephesians 1:3-12
[33] Philippians 3:12 (paraphrased)

6.

Regardless of the timing of this season, it is the foundation of Convergence, for in it we get to know the essence of God's character. In many ways this is the logical place to start. Nowadays there is an increased spiritual openness, but some of it is faith in faith itself. Faith in God is directed and grounded faith: directed towards the person of Jesus, and grounded in a knowledge of his person and "work." For some, "faith" is marked by "the introduction."

> "Jesus Christ, Mr. Jones."
> "Mr. Jones, Jesus Christ."

Knowing God. This is an exciting season.

THE CHARACTER OF GOD

In our quest to live a life of faith, we need to know in whom we are placing our faith.[34] One hindrance to moving toward Convergence is that our concept of God is too small. He is not the all-powerful, creation-calling, sea-splitting, smoke-billowing, fire-falling, nation-naming, water-walking, death-defying, Life-living God of the Bible. We have shrunk him into someone we can safely understand and, better yet, contain.

But why risk our lives for one who is not all-knowing, unquestionably good, undeniably able, and infinitely informed? The

---

[34] The New International Version Christian Growth Study Bible covers the topic of God's character well in its endnotes.

faith

shrink-wrapped Savior we have sometimes espoused has little appeal to a world hungry for the authentic God of the Universe.

Pause for a moment and ask two questions: Which of these characteristics of God do I think are most important (✓)? and Which characteristics do I most exhibit?

❏ Holy	❏ Just	❏ Faithful
❏ Love	❏ Gracious	❏ Kind
❏ Gentle	❏ Good	❏ Patient
❏ Passionate	❏ Committed	❏ Caring
❏ Light	❏ Joyful	❏ Peaceful
❏ Everywhere/Present	❏ All-powerful	❏ All-knowing
❏ Jealous	❏ Great	❏ _____
❏ _____	❏ _____	❏ _____

As we get to understand the character of God, by faith, then a host of questions spring to mind.

• If God is all these things (and I am created in his likeness), why am I not more like him?
• And what else is there about this God that I don't know?

So we begin to go through an intense period of discovering God, and having our presuppositions and actions challenged to the core. Given the fact that God is infinite and we are imperfect, this process never ends.

MY PERSONAL STORY

In the small community of Llandudno just 20 miles south of Cape Town on the Atlantic side of South Africa, the church was, to our family, the center of life. In fact, like the local school, the church started in our home.

My Dad and Mom were business people. But they were more than that. They were strongly bi-vocational. I never heard them use that language, but I watched them preach, teach, superintend Sunday Schools, run youth groups and manage the affairs of the local church. There was no full-time pastor until J.L. Green, a Baptist Minister, retired and came to live in Llandudno. He was my grandfather.

It wasn't a hotly evangelical or a swing-from-the-chandeliers charismatic church, but it was church. Perhaps not surprisingly I grew up with a dichotomy: I knew what was right, but I didn't find myself doing it. In Llandudno "those Johnson boys" were accused of many of the maladies common to any village. Broken windows, fruit stealing, whatever. Some of it was even true. On Sundays we were angels; the rest of the week we were just boys.

But we were churchy boys. I taught Sunday School from age 13, led a Bible Study in my boarding school every Wednesday night from age 14 (half the hostel professed a personal relationship with Jesus Christ), began co-leading a Youth for Christ club at age 18. I was christened, confirmed, inoculated and membered. I knew much about God, but didn't know him personally.

One night, at the same City Hall in Cape Town where years before my grandmother had sung with the Cape Town Symphony Orchestra, our youth group was at a rally. The preacher, Dr. Frank Retief, said that when the crowds followed Jesus but later turned away, it was for one of three reasons:

(1) their **motives** in following him were wrong (Give us bread);
(2) their **understanding** of him was wrong (He'd be a political conqueror), or
(3) their **repentance** wasn't real.

Now I was trying to follow Christ for the right reasons. I knew there was something more to life that I didn't have. I had seen plenty and want, and wasn't after the goodies. And I knew the synoptic gospels, the Gospel Light Sunday School materials, and the major and minor prophets by the time I was 13. But I came up short when it got to the bit about repentance.

By the time I was 18 or 19 years old, I was frustrated. I was trying to be a Christian. I went to Christian meetings. (I led many of them.) I read my Bible diligently. Yet I had no peace. I was striving to find God. But I wasn't finding him anywhere very fast.

Repentance is a strange thing. It's a word we avoid...like sin, conviction and commitment. The strange part is that it's a simple choice, a 180-degree turning around. But it requires that God show us our need to turn. And I was probably more self-righteous than a 100 person church choir.

I'm not sure how it happened, but shortly after that evening at the Cape Town City Hall, I knelt at my desk, and had a peek into my own heart. And it was not a pretty sight. I felt that for the first time I saw myself as God saw me, and my need for a heart change became all too apparent. Through no work of my own, I moved from remorse to repentance. Things I had known intellectually to be wrong, I now had a heart-felt loathing for. The miraculous gift of forgiveness was given and received.

Like countless numbers before me, from then on my reading of scripture took on new life. The Book was in color. I could begin to live from the inside out. I didn't just know about God, I knew him.

DIFFERENT NAMES, DIFFERENT SITUATIONS

Putting a label on the "faith experience" is problematic. Too little definition and we leave people in a verbal fog. Too many clichés and ABCs and people genuinely seeking to follow Jesus are disqualified in our minds because they don't know all the right jargon. But do we? What did Jesus say about our response to him? And what did he call people who responded appropriately? Here are some examples.

Situation or person	What Jesus said	References
Simon and Andrew	"Come, follow me."	Mark 1:17
James and John	Without delay he called them, and they left their father Zebedee in the boat with the hired men and followed him.	Mark 1:20
Levi, son of Alphaeus	"Follow me."	Mark 2:14
Rich young man	"Go, sell everything you have and give to the poor, and you will have treasure in heaven. Then come, follow me."	Mark 10:21
Blind Bartimaeus	"Go, your faith has healed you."	Mark 10:52
Teacher of the law	"You are not far from the kingdom of God."	Mark 12:34

What did Jesus call his followers?

Situation or person	What Jesus said	References
Crowds	Salt of the earth, light of the world	Matthew 5:13,14
Peter and Andrew	Fishers of men	Matthew 4:19
Sick woman	Daughter	Matthew 9:22
Sending out of "the twelve"	Disciples (Matthew's name for them, not Jesus')	Matthew 10:1
Disciples	Students	Matthew 10:24
Jesus instructing his followers	"Whoever acknowledges me..."	Matthew 10:32
When disciples told Jesus that his natural family was there	"Whoever does the will of my father in heaven is my brother and sister and mother."	Matthew 12:34

We often hear it said, "Become a Christian" or "Join the church" or "Follow these four steps and you will know Jesus/be saved." But is Scripture asking us to become a Christian (with all of the historical baggage that the term can carry)? No. We are being asked to follow Jesus.

Did Jesus ever say "You must become a Christian?" Not once. The label "Christian" wasn't even used in a positive context. How did believers in the early Church describe themselves? Usually as "followers" or "followers of the Way."

In most translations the word "Christian" appears two or three times. It is unclear whether the word was one chosen by the followers of Jesus, or one that was placed upon them by those who didn't care much for their beliefs. Either way, today "Christian" is a loaded term that can create unnecessary barriers for people who simply want a relationship with Jesus Christ. We must be careful that the labels we use don't become obstacles for knowing Jesus. We must also be careful to not prescribe formulae that even Jesus did not impose on those who sought to know him.

THE CRUX OF THE MATTER

A young man and his sister came to see me some years ago. She was unsure of her relationship with Jesus and wanted some counsel. I pulled out my list of verses on *assurance of salvation* and gave her a long pep talk. But I made the grave mistake of never making sure that she had actually made a decision to follow Jesus. I never asked whether she believed the historical truth that the God-man, Jesus, had paid a price for her separation from God. I did not make sure that she had accepted his free gift of forgiveness for her sins. I did not stop to make sure that the moment of spiritual regeneration had actually taken place. I talked long and hard, as I recall, about the things she had to do to live like a believer. I never did probe the simple question: has the eternal transaction actually taken place? It wasn't long before she drifted into doing her own thing.

A lot of spiritual-sounding stuff is floating around the marketplace today. Most of it masks the historical fact that Jesus chose to die on a cross to take the punishment for our wrongdoing. He died so that our misdemeanors could be forgiven. Then he was buried. After three days he came alive again and lives today to share a brand new type of life with us. This is God's plan. Our part is to decide whether we buy into this free plan. In our day of self-help, personal empowerment and I-want-to-be-in-control, there is this stark truth:

> The message that points to Christ on the cross seems like sheer silliness to those hell-bent on destruction, but for those on the way of salvation it makes perfect sense. This is the way God works, and most powerfully as it turns out.[35]

Try to find a smarter way if you like, but Christ crucified is God's best and only plan.

FOLLOWING JESUS

The key to the season of faith is not the orderly arrangement of religious verbiage, but the deep alignment of our whole being with objective truth. It is easier to straighten a bone just after it has been broken. It is often easier for the Great Surgeon to straighten out damaged lives on the heels of the transformational experience of first coming to know him. On the shores of Galilee fishermen were called to become disciples. Discipleship involves discipline. And the season of faith extends to include the establishing of transformational disciplines in our daily routine:

- Worship: ascribing worth to God above all else
- Bible reading: renewing our thinking to become like God's
- Prayer: re-establishing daily conversations that were lost in the Garden of Eden
- Fasting: saying *No* to the temporal and *Yes* to the eternal

There are other disciplines like these and many fine writings about them. The point here is that the deliberateness, discipline and conviction of the first steps we take during the season of faith often determine the likelihood of our coming to Convergence.

Search the Bible, and expect a few surprises as you enjoy your season of Faith. And remember that it is not a summer vacation season, but the laying of foundations upon which much will depend in future seasons.

---

[35] I Corinthians 1:23-25, Eugene H. Peterson, *The Message*, NavPress, 1994

NOT WITHOUT OPPOSITION

Another use of the word *Christian* is in 1 Peter 4:16 where Peter says "Yet if *anyone suffers* as a Christian, let him not be ashamed, but let him glorify God in this matter."

We would be remiss to close this chapter without pointing out that new believers have entered a war zone. A continuous battle wages over the lives of individuals seriously pursuing God.

Using the tapestry analogy, there is a war for the loom and a struggle over the shuttle: who will be in control—God, Satan or us? There are constant assaults on the threads: tear them, twist them, and sidetrack them. There is the inevitable introduction of threads that are not included in God's design, be they from us or Satan "just wanting to add a little color" or give God a hand. There is the delay tactic: weave it later, let the shuttle lie still, relax for a while... when you have made more money/had more experience/seen a bit more of the world.

The road to Convergence is chosen at a price. It involves tough decisions, and the right decisions are sometimes the result of battles. (Other decisions seem easy, particularly if they are the result of God's more visible sovereignty when we are left with little choice. More about this in the next chapter.) We will do battle with ourselves and our circumstances—"the godly in Christ shall suffer"[36]—particularly as God combs through the tangles of our lives and brings them into alignment with himself.

We can have two equal but opposite errors: being preoccupied with Satan, and being unaware of his schemes. Know your God, know yourself, and know your enemy.

---

[36] 2 Timothy 3:12 "In fact, everyone who wants to live a godly life in Christ Jesus will be persecuted..."

7.

Those who fear God, hear God. This is true for all people. What is not so clear is the manner in which we hear the invisible God speak to his creation.

LOOKING BACK

It was one of those special moments. Lyn and I were flying back from Washington D.C. having witnessed perhaps the largest gathering of men in history on the National Mall.[37] On top of this, we had just signed a Letter of Intent to move forward in a partnership with University of the Nations on the development of a leadership and research center just south of Kona, Hawaii. On the return to San Francisco at 30,000 feet Lyn and I began to list the major decisions we had made in our almost 25 years together. Starting to date each other, Lyn's first job, getting married, buying our first home, taking a trip to Europe when we didn't have the money, taking another trip six months later to Chile... still no money. Having children, moving to America, staying in America, spending $375,000 on a fixer-upper. Several job transitions...

We asked ourselves what the dominant factors were in each decision. It was a holy moment (lasting two or three hours). Slowly the patterns began to emerge. With me, the still, small voice. With

---

[37] On October 4, 1997 perhaps as many as one million men gathered in a sacred assembly to repent, pray and commit themselves to the principles of godly character. This Promise Keepers event moved us as we witnessed people kneeling, standing and sitting before God in prayer.

Decision	Dominant factor	Other factor	Result	Primary mover
Salvation	Bible preached (Brett)	Believers	Conversion	Holy Spirit
Career • initial choice • where to study • first job	Still small voice	Basic research	Job at Price Waterhouse	Brett
Dating	Desires of hearts	Match of gifts	Began dating, October 5th, '75	Lyn!
First Home	Desires of our heart	Impulse (Ps. 37:4)	Bought first home (before we were married)	Lyn
Starting a family	Lyn: ready for this stage of life Brett: not ready—God had to do heart surgery	Prodding from friend ("You better ask God why you aren't ready...)	Fay Maree born March 29, '83	Lyn, later Brett
Trips to Chile, Austria	Others: offer from Lyn's parents to accompany them	Circumstances (rented out house for summer to get money)	Great vacation in Europe	Elton and Cynthia Moller
Coming to the States	The trip: Price Waterhouse The location: "God, where should we go?"	Timing: readiness of church, pregnancy with son, James	Came to San Francisco June 1986 (for one year)	Sovereignty. I had no way of knowing that choosing SF was God's plan; he worked out the details.
Buying the Belmont house	Impulse (Lyn and Fay)	Our children, our friends	Bought $375,000 house with -$1,000 in the bank	Lyn
Starting Creative Memories	Impulse (Lyn and Fay)	Brett's prayer	Started successful business	Lyn
Brett leaving Price Waterhouse	Still, small voice	Circumstances (couldn't afford to stay)	New career at KPMG	Brett
Leaving KPMG Peat Marwick	God's whisper; sensing a new season	Family priorities	Different type of skills building season at CSC	Brett
Starting e-Quip (Professionals for Christ)	Vision, Call	Gifting	A non-profit that bridges the world of Career and Call	Brett

Decision	Dominant factor	Other factor	Result	Primary mover
Starting The Institute	Asking stupid questions: "God, got any good ideas?"	Prompting of wife; godly counsel of friends	A new type of vehicle for ministry	Brett and Lyn
Partnering on King's Mansion with a missions organization	Trusted friends	Witness of the Spirit	New blend of business and missions	Others, us
Moving to San Carlos	Impulse, generosity	Our children	A house move	Us

Lyn, the impulse. For me, the restlessness and an unfolding of "the big picture." For Lyn, just the picture. For both of us, confirming scriptures. As we progressed through each decision we made a grid so that we could better understand God's ways with us.

What was also clear to us was that sometimes neither of us was going to "get it." No matter how hard we prayed or dreamed or thought, we were not going to envisage the broader plan that God had in mind. So God just had to do something in his sovereignty, usually creating circumstances over which we had no control. For example, when buying our first house the mortgage broker made an error on early calculations leading us to believe we could actually afford the house, and our "one year trip" to the U.S. which has, so far, become a thirteen year "trip."

PRINCIPLES OF HEARING GOD

Others have written well on principles of hearing God. Because hearing God is so crucial to following his initiative, some reminders are worth mentioning:

- **Understand past patterns of guidance in your life.** Don't go with the standard experiences of others; examine your own walk to uncover the Infinite God's ways with you.
- **Open your life to your spouse.** God in his fairness will sometimes provide key points of guidance only through your husband or wife. Part of this is his way of ensuring that you remain inter-dependent. It is easy to

slip into the habit of sharing your needs with people other than your life-mate. The excitement of talking to someone who doesn't know you but finds you interesting can be intoxicating. The downside of this habit is that when a big decision comes along and you need guidance, God may be hiding it in your wife or husband, yet you have blunted the cutting edge of hearing God together.

- **Listen for God in children.** This is true for children generally, but it is especially true that he speaks to us through our own children. We are not advocating that parents be held hostage to the whims of their children, but too often we fail to ask God to speak to us through our kids, particularly as they grow older. Natural pressures pull teenagers away from this role in the family (like thinking that their parents are IQ-deprived). Stick with it; children often hear God clearly. We once received a request from the twelve-year-old daughter of missionary friends. She was raising support for a summer of working in an orphanage in Eastern Europe. We asked the children to pray with us about how much we should give. I was thinking $50 would be plenty but Fay who was nine at the time announced that we should give $150. ("Why $150?" the rest of us asked. "I saw a check with $150 written on it flying through the sky.") Their young girl was all packed and ready to go although without her full fees, she could not leave. Within an hour or two of her departure, our check arrived. She needed exactly $150.

- **Open your life to others.** This may appear to be the paradox of the previous points. The fact is that we need both our spouse and others; in that order. The confirmation, if not the impetus, often comes from the outside.

- **Be prepared to "go to the mat" alone with God to find out what he has to say about a situation or decision.** At times our Father wants us to wait things out with him. This is his prerogative. I have experienced a number of times when he spoke to me, and I sensed that going to others would have been a sad breach of God's confidence. "Wait for God. Wait patiently for him to act." When our precious daughter had the alarming signs of a seizure we went to God in desperate prayer. The doctors wanted to perform a series of sleep-deprivation tests to reinduce the condition so that they could observe her. In and of themselves the tests might have been harmful. As a father I went to my Father deeply concerned. After some time I felt God say, "In two years she will be completely healed." Many times we would hear her in the night, get to her, and observe that she was having another seizure. It was a long two years, but she was indeed healed and there has been not so much as a hint of another seizure.

- **Communicate constantly.** "Pray without ceasing." Ask God about the little things. Hearing him speak about small things builds faith for the larger challenges that will come.
- **Separate the short-term (near-term) from the long-term.** Understand timing.

If you used to hear God but have not known his guidance for a while:

- Go back to where you last clearly heard God's voice. Perhaps God has asked you to do something that you need to follow through on.
- Consider whether you are in the desert. If so, look for relationship, not lots of forward direction.
- Acknowledge and turn away from any known sin. (Ps. 66:18)
- Make sure you are not responding negatively to the situations God is placing in your life. He sometimes uses the unpleasant to accomplish his plans. Suffering produces perseverance, perseverance character, character hope, and hope lets us "see" the love of God in our lives.[38]

THE WILD WAYS SOME FOLK HEAR GOD

Ask a group of people how God speaks to them. Really. We've been taught some pat answers, and they're good. Through the Word, counselors, etc. But isn't God infinite? And isn't he the essence of creativity? And isn't communication at the essence of his being? Likewise there is a diversity of ways in which he speaks to his children today. God could speak to you in ways he's never done before!

Lyn gave a talk at a church and asked the participants to list the ways in which God speaks to them. Some of this may be familiar to you. We have categorized the lists and added a few things that we have known to be true in the lives of friends.

[38]Romans 5

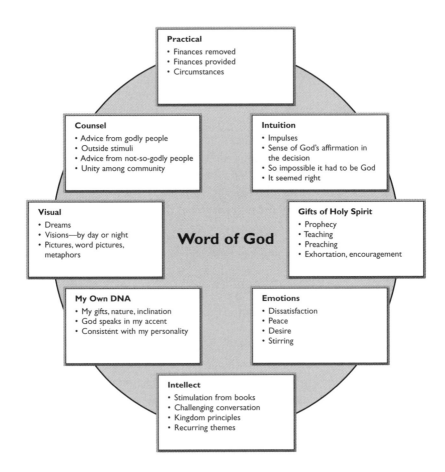

Practical
- Finances removed
- Finances provided
- Circumstances

Counsel
- Advice from godly people
- Outside stimuli
- Advice from not-so-godly people
- Unity among community

Intuition
- Impulses
- Sense of God's affirmation in the decision
- So impossible it had to be God
- It seemed right

Visual
- Dreams
- Visions—by day or night
- Pictures, word pictures, metaphors

Word of God

Gifts of Holy Spirit
- Prophecy
- Teaching
- Preaching
- Exhortation, encouragement

My Own DNA
- My gifts, nature, inclination
- God speaks in my accent
- Consistent with my personality

Emotions
- Dissatisfaction
- Peace
- Desire
- Stirring

Intellect
- Stimulation from books
- Challenging conversation
- Kingdom principles
- Recurring themes

exercises

Look up the verses listed below and make your own observations about the ways in which God spoke to people in Bible times.

Verse	How God Spoke	True for you?
Genesis 41		
Exodus 37:1-5		
I Kings 19:12		
Numbers 22:28		
Job 33:14-29		
Joel 33:14-29		
Joel 2:28		
Psalm 19:1		
Psalm 37:4		
Psalm 119:105		
Habakkuk 2:1-3		
John 16:13-15		
Colossians 3:15		
Hebrews 2:1-2		

RUN THAT ONE THROUGH THE FUNNEL

We are constantly bombarded with messages and words. How do we filter what we hear to discern whether it is from God?

The picture of the funnel is a series of filters with three major sections through which we "run" our decisions:

- ❏ Compliance: does this comply with the broad strokes of the written Word of God, what God has already spoken to me, and who he has created me to be?
- ❏ Community: how does it affect others? What do they have to say about the matter?
- ❏ Commitment: are we/am I willing and able to commit the resources suggested by this decision?

A word about the "Community" piece of the filter: the evangelical tradition of the past 150 years or so has emphasized the notion of "personal salvation" and the importance of the individual's relationship with Jesus. While this is true, it is not the whole truth. Further, it is not the dominant truth of the New Testament or Old Testament for that matter. Walking out the life of Jesus in us—being a follower of the Way—was never intended to be a "just Jesus and you" experience as the old song suggests. The Community filters therefore need to be considered carefully.

Hearing God is often a matter of learning to ask the right questions, expecting that he hears, listens and answers. Let's take a closer look at some of the filters.

Filter	Questions to Consider	
Word of God	• Is it consistent with the written Word of God? • Has God already spoken to us on this subject? Have we obeyed what he said?	**C O M P L I A N C E**
Your Values	• Is it consistent with my Values (and my philosophy of ministry)? • How does it reinforce these values?	
Your Purpose, Call or Vision	• Does it move me in the same direction as my call? Or is it a divergence? • How does it underscore or clarify the vision God has given me?	
Consistency with gifts or talents	We have listed this as a "major filter" even though at times it is less important. For example, during the Skills Building season when we are discovering our gifts and adding to our toolbox, it can be less important to have an exact fit. "Whatever your hand finds to do, do it with all your might" can be more appropriate. • For sustainability, however, we do well to ask, Is this consistent with my gifts and talents? • If I do not have the skills, is this an opportunity to grow skills I need?	
Consideration for others	• Who are the key stakeholders? How are they affected? What is the cost to them? A note of caution: there are critical junctures on our journey when God asks us to obey him and not hide behind the cost to others. This should be sensitively factored into our decision-making.	**C O M M U N I T Y**
Unity among all stakeholders	• Is there agreement? If there is not unanimity of thinking, is there at least a "unity of the Spirit"? • Have we tested for alignment among stakeholders? How? • Do we need to consider our roles and responsibilities should the decision go through?	
Action	• Are we committed to the action this decision demands? • Do we have a short-term or long-term view? What does this decision require of us?	**C O M M I T M E N T**
Grace	• Will I have the grace? • Does my "grace barometer" soar or leak on the floor? • God's smile; is there a settled-ness beyond what the circumstances might suggest?	
Margin	• Does it sap or supply margin? • Do I have the resources, or what are the alternate resources? • Am I willing to make trade-offs to increase margin?	
Timing	• Is the timing right? Should we wait? • Is this the right decision for this season of my life? • Are there prerequisites that need to be set in place first?	

After all this filtering of the avalanche of rocks and rubble and mud, we are left with the diamonds.

FEARING GOD

It's fun to talk about how God still speaks to us today. No doubt some people will take exception to this, but for me it is no problem that the one from whom all communication flows is still communicating. Interaction is wired into the Godhead—three-in-one cannot help but communicate.

Some of us seem to have more "words from the Lord" in a week than some authentic saints have in a lifetime. (God said this, then he said that...) This might disturb some, but what should concern us more is the absence of a true Fear of God in our lives. Many of us make plans and decisions as if life were simply ours to decide and live. We can also gradually tighten the circle of things about which we allow God to speak to us. The inevitable result is a lack of Convergence.

Am I saying that an absence of Convergence is an indication of a lack of fearing God? Absolutely not. I am saying that an absence of the Fear of God will stunt Convergence. If we do not fear God, we lessen the chances that we will know his leading.

In *The Joy of Fearing God*[39] Jerry Bridges subscribes to the common definition of the Fear of God, namely, reverential awe. Why does it take a book to unpack this topic? In part because we have become so familiar with God that we lose sight of his awesome greatness. In our quest for Abba-intimacy, we forget he is the King of Kings.

[39] Jerry Bridges, *The Joy of Fearing God*, Waterbrook Press, 1975

• Take 10 minutes to skim through the book of Proverbs and list as many of the advantages of Fearing God as you can find.

• Review the characteristics of God (repeated from an earlier chapter) and consider which of these could contribute to a healthy Fear of God.

❏ Holy	❏ Just	❏ Faithful
❏ Love	❏ Gracious	❏ Kind
❏ Gentle	❏ Good	❏ Patient
❏ Passionate	❏ Committed	❏ Caring
❏ Light	❏ Joyful	❏ Peaceful
❏ Everywhere/Present	❏ All-powerful	❏ All-knowing
❏ Jealous	❏ Great	❏ _____
❏ _____	❏ _____	❏ _____

ALTERNATIVES TO FEARING GOD

What are some of the alternatives to fearing God?

• Fearing man, but remember that, "the fear of man brings a snare."
• Doing our own thing; leaning on our own understanding.
• Fearing our circumstances (seeing evil coming when it is not really there).
• Fearing the future.
• Fearing change.

Paul gives Timothy some counsel that is much needed in a world where doctors' offices are overflowing with people who are filled with fear.

> "God has not given us a spirit of fear, but of power, of love and a sound mind (self-discipline)"[40]

Convergence is, in part, the outcome of lots of small decisions. Decisions are often directly related to our ability to hear God. Hearing God is linked to fearing God.

> Now what I am commanding you today is not too difficult for you or beyond your reach. It is not up in heaven, so that you have to ask, "Who will ascend into heaven to get it and proclaim it to us so that we may obey it?" Nor is it beyond the sea, so that you have to ask, "Who will cross the sea to get it and proclaim it to us so we may obey it?" No, the word is very near you: it is in your mouth and in your heart so that you may obey it.[41]

ROUTINE RESPONSIVENESS

Look at this through the window of responsibility or responsiveness to God. Scripture indicates that we will know God's will when we plan to obey God's will.[42] For the most part, God will speak to us (consistently, in a growth mode) when he sees "routine responsiveness" in our lives. This is not to say that we are perfect, only that we are willing, despite our unbelief and inability to follow through. Because of the importance of routine responsiveness to God's voice, accountability can make an enormous difference in one's walk to Convergence. It is a rare person who stays the course without others holding him or her accountable for the best use of God's gifts. One question we should ask each other is: Are we keeping a soft posture towards God's desires for our lives?

[40] 2 Timothy 1:7 Note that scripture sometimes sees fear as a spirit. In extreme cases of fear, we do well to recognize the spiritual forces at work and deal with them appropriately.
[41] Deut. 30:11-14
[42] John 8:29-32

Consider major decisions in your life and what the patterns have been. List five big decisions you have made and the factors that led you towards each decision.

Decision	Dominant factor	Other factor	Result	Primary mover

8.

The self-help sections of bookstores are brimming with books that promise to build you up in every possible way. Unfortunately, their premise is that you can make yourself whatever you want to be. The self-help view puts us at the center; God's view has him at the center and encourages us to discover and exercise, within the context of a relationship with the Godhead, the gifts he has given us. Discovering our gifts involves lots of trial and error; those who do well in this season are those who *do*.

Personally, I didn't know myself until I knew God. Young people seem to try on different personae like clothes at a shopping mall. "Is this me? Does it fit?" This process is healthy and normal. It is also subject to certain risks. If we are not content with who we are and are not secure in the love of Jesus, there is the danger that we'll fashion images of ourselves designed to mask the cracks. Further, we cultivate some notion that we are people of our own creation. If we are particularly pleased with who we are (which probably means that we haven't seen ourselves as God sees us) we become proud. If we don't like the end product, we reject ourselves. Worse still, we cut ourselves off from the wonderful process of discovering how our Creator fashioned us. Since the Garden of Eden, God has enjoyed sharing his creativity with man. Discovering your own gifts is a wonderful continuation of that process.

discovering your gifts

PRINCIPLES OF GIFT DISCOVERY

Recently I discussed with a psychologist friend the wide variety of personality profiling tools on the market. He cautioned that most of these tests are designed to meet the needs of the researchers and not those filling out the forms. The "Sophie's Choice" questionnaires do not always yield a fair result. ("Would you rather keep your daughter or your son"-type questions sometimes leave one without a fair answer. "Neither" would render you indecisive, of course.) We have made no attempt to duplicate the many tests that are available; they are widely known and can be very helpful. Instead we offer 10 simple steps to get you on the road to gift discovery.

1. **Find a need and fill it.** Particularly in your early years, try to do a variety of things. Don't wait for the perfect job or the ideal assignment. Park some cars, copy cassette tapes, change a diaper or two.
2. **Develop a willingness to serve.** Don't let your ability outstrip your availability.
3. **"Don't think of yourself more highly than you ought."**[43] In an age where young people (and not so young) seem to be taught more about packaging than content, don't believe your own press reports. Develop a healthy skepticism for your own opinions. As a modern sage has said, the goldfish doesn't always have the best perspective of the fish bowl.
4. **Take a good gift identification test...**
5. **...but don't get pigeon-holed.** Meyers Briggs did not write the Bible.
6. **Get older mentors...**
7. **...and avoid those who assume you lack gifts because you are young.**
8. **Ignore character development in your pursuit of gift development...at your own peril.**
9. **Be part of a team.** The Bible calls it a body. The Lone Ranger had some glorious moments on his own, but when the going got tough, it was "we." You won't discover your gifts without discovering your dependence on others.
10. **Be more concerned with obedience than career.** As Campbell McAlpine said, "There are more crises of obedience than guidance."

---

[43] Romans 12:3

A SEASON, NOT A TEST

Just in case we are beginning to sound formulaic, remember gift discovery is a season. I spent about 10 years developing and discovering my gifts. I had a running joke with a friend with whom I had the privilege of co-working for about five years.

When we taught ten- and eleven-year-olds Sunday School he said, "You should never stop doing this. You are gifted with this age group." Shortly thereafter, I stopped teaching that class and he took it over. A while later he again said words to the effect of, "You should never stop teaching youth group. You are gifted at leading teenagers." It wasn't long before my ten or so years of leading youth were over. Some time later, after we had pastored a church together, he said "You should stay with the local church and I should go and do missions." I knew it was time to start packing. It wasn't long before we left Hout Bay, South Africa and came to the San Francisco Bay Area.

Was my friend misguided? Not at all. It's just that sometimes, particularly when we are young, we see a talent as our life-long Call, when God sees it as an opportunity to grow our gifts. "Whatever you do, do it with all your might." But remember, you may just be doing it for a season.

While this is true, there is a corollary: God is not trying to get us through a pipeline of seasons; he is trying to get us. Period. No matter what season we are in, the issue is not the passage of time, but our preparation.

GIFT TESTS

A variety of tests have been designed to help us discover our gifts.

- Find one that suits you and use it to better understand what your gifts look like on paper.
- Obtain input on your gifts and strengths from friends or acquaintances.
- Then look for a place to serve, and discover what your gifts are (or are not) in practice. We discover what is right by practicing doing right.

THE LEMON MODEL OF LEADERSHIP

As a new believer I attended leadership training courses, read the recommended reading, and proceeded to do what leaders do. It wasn't bad stuff, but it suggested a singular view of leadership that is not only unreal, but robs unconventional leaders of their place in life.

In the world of business, much of the leadership literature focuses on two categories: Entrepreneurs and Managers. Within the latter category there is some dissection to deal with the differences between what are fondly called "executives" and "general managers."

I have observed numerous leadership difficulties get described as "personality conflicts" for want of a better explanation as to why a leadership team did not get along. The heart of the issue is that our models for defining a leader are incomplete. We desperately force people into too few boxes, and then label only some of the boxes L-E-A-D-E-R.

From my work with clients and colleagues I have settled on five types of leadership. Before we review these, note that each category is a category of leadership; in other words, all are leaders. They simply lead from a different perspective. We have named this the LEMON Model of Leadership.[44]

Type of Leader	Characteristics	Locus of Leadership
Luminary	• Believe that ideas precede activities • Thought leaders: value concepts and fresh thinking. Create their own "hand" • Often long range thinkers • Can be prophetic • Inspire organizations through the power of their ideas • Sometimes stay "above" practical, day-to-day tasks • Care more about why than how	Ideas

[44] The LEMON Model of Leadership is a Trademark of I⁴ International

Type of Leader	Characteristics	Locus of Leadership
Entrepreneur	• Believe that opportunities precede activities • Opportunists: make the most of whatever hand they are dealt • Short-to-medium term thinkers • Visionaries, but shorter term than Luminaries • Inspire organizations through energy and enthusiasm • Will do any tasks in the early phases of the venture • Care more about results • See "failure" as learning experiences • Can envision and create something out of nothing	Opportunities
Manager	• Believe that proper planning precedes activities • Deliberate: will patiently change the hand they are dealt • Long-term thinkers • Implementers of vision • Build organizational loyalty through proven results • Will build a team to get tasks done rather than do the tasks themselves • Understand process, planning, profits • Do not like "failure" as it makes them seem like they haven't done their homework	Systems
Organizer	• Action oriented • Have an "unconscious competence": they intuitively pick the right things to focus on • Feel they have nothing to teach on management • Verbal communicators • Can be suspicious of plans and reports • Love to bring things "to a close" • A quick result is the best result (usually always) • Good at identifying Issues, but weak on formulating Vision	Loyalty to leader
Networker	• People oriented • Love to bring people together • Instinctively build networks... • ...Even if they are not always sure what to do with them • Can be vague on purpose • "If we get enough smart people in the room, the right thing is sure to happen." • Verbal communicators... • ...but not consistent communicators • Even their communications are "event driven" • Good at gathering people, but not necessarily strong on strategy	Connecting People

None of us is solely one type of leader or another. A few people are a good blend of three or four of these categories. The LEMON Model of Leadership is included here, not to box you into a category, but to open you up to thinking more broadly about yourself and your leadership.

HINDRANCES TO GIFT DISCOVERY

The top seven reasons why we don't discover our gifts:

1. We do not have a context that is calling out, coaching, and applauding our gifts.
2. We are waiting for the "perfect" job to come along.
3. We are willing to serve, but not yet. (Procrastination.)
4. We are not willing to serve. (False advertising tells us we can start at the top...without having to pay our dues.)
5. Schedule-pressure and fatigue. (This is particularly true during the teenage years when children are asked to keep the daily schedules of adults, and still have time to discover who they are.)
6. Internal insecurity causes us to shrink from trying. (Insecurity can cause us to (a) put down the gifts of others so that we feel better about ourselves, or (b) undermine our own gifts.)
7. An inadequate understanding of the different types of gifts.

exercises

- Consider the types of leaders listed in the LEMON Model of Leadership above and highlight the characteristics that sound like you.

- Review the list of hindrances, and consider which of these may be applicable to you.

9.

What do you do when no one is looking? Who are you when no one else is around? How would you respond under pressure to comply, give in, conform? Do you really know? Can we ever know for sure?

As in many things, there are two seemingly opposing perspectives on these questions. We are taught, "Let him who thinks he stands take heed lest he fall." On the other hand, sometimes God needs to assure us that he has, perhaps over a long process, built character into us. He wants us to have a level of certainty, not so we can be proud, but so that we can have the courage to cooperate with him in new ventures.

MORE THAN A JIFFY LUBE CHECKUP

We'd like to check this season off our list quite quickly. Judging by the experience of men and women who were close followers of God in history, it's usually not that simple. Somehow when it comes to the seasons of Skills Building and Internal Integrity, God's timetable is slow and relaxed. Later in this section we will review a few characters who knew this to be true.

Back in the mid-1980s, I attempted to launch a consulting practice in a new area of thought. "Executive information systems" were hot—or at least the market predictions looked that way. Price Waterhouse had agreed that we should pursue the practice, and I had decided that it wouldn't hurt if I was a nationally-known speaker. A software company approached me to do a road show in 17 major North American cities to launch their new product. It was a great opportunity.

Naturally I had to clear it with the folks at "Corporate." I spoke to a colleague who assured me that he had cleared it with the partner-in-charge, and I could go ahead. I sensed a check in my spirit—was everything okay?—but went ahead anyway.

After all of the invitations were printed with my name on them and many distributed across the country, all hell broke loose. Price Waterhouse had signed a national alliance with another software company that they deemed to be a competitor of the company I was working with, and the partner-in-charge was livid.

Daily interrogations. Unpleasant phone calls. People questioning my integrity. After the first few days I implored God to ease up. I had learned my lesson. Enough was enough. But it continued for a month or more. I felt as if God had his foot on my neck, and I had the sense he was in no rush to remove it until the lessons of listening to God and not giving him a helping hand were baked into my being.

A SEASON, NOT A SENTENCE

Less-than-pleasant times are not always the result of punishment. If this were the case, we would spend our lives avoiding difficulties to stay "in God's will." Apart from an observation of scripture, my experience is that God leads us into tough times. It's true that he does not tempt us to sin (James 1). He does lead us into difficulties.

At about 24 years of age, I had the privilege of pastoring a wonderful group of people. The job wasn't one I chose—it was more like a wartime "field promotion," which is what happens when the guy in front of you gets shot. With a very committed team of volunteers, we re-built a local church over a five-year period. By many accounts, it was a successful venture.

By 1990 I had moved to the United States. We were approached by a group of people who wanted to meet for fellowship. All of them had been in some position of church leadership; some had participated faithfully in foreign missions. It should have been easy. For months we spent social time, worshipped and prayed together. Then some in the group felt that we should start a church (rather than just be the church). Posters, flyers, rented space...the whole deal.

For a variety of reasons it never happened. On top of this, the fellowship group folded. In short, it was a failure. While it's a longer story than I have explained, the questions remain: Were we led into this experience? Did God want us to fail? I think so. Bob Mumford says "There is nothing quite so dangerous as a string of unbroken success."

Tests of our integrity are needed to make us strong. And they don't always come because we messed up. Often, it's to the contrary.

OUT-JACOBING JACOB

We have established that God is not vindictive. At times, however, things are rooted deep in our being that require uprooting. Often the infinitely creative God uses the University of the Desert to heal us of these maladies, but sometimes he lets us get outdone by someone who is like us. If we are not prepared to hate our own sin, we seem to be willing to hate it in others, and then, by grace, recognize that we are riddled with the same thing. Jacob knew all about this.

Jacob was a schemer.[45] He was the quintessential entrepreneur. By hook or by crook he would find an angle. And it's not that God wasn't in some of the schemes. But when Jacob hatched a plan to make Rachel his wife, Laban, his would-be father-in-law, outdid him.[46] When Jacob planned an escape, Laban cut him off at the pass. This sparring went on for 14 years. Jacob lunged, Laban ducked. Eventually Jacob left with much material wealth—not everything always goes bad at once—but he still had to face a past nemesis. En route to see his brother, God met Jacob. The culmi-

---

[45] Genesis 27
[46] Genesis 29 - 33

nation of a 14-year Internal Integrity project resulted in a struggle with God. Jacob passed the test, but in the process he was forever marked. Thereafter the self-made achiever walked with a limp.

We are only really safe to do God's bidding when we walk with a limp. Furthermore, I am convinced that we cannot come to Convergence until we limp from having been broken by God. Before this point, we say we will never deny him. After this point, we are less cocky about ourselves and have a more tender heart for our Lord Jesus.

"Blessed are those who know they are poor in spirit."

• Consider the nature of the Internal Integrity tests in the lives of the following leaders:

Leader	Reference	Internal Integrity tests
Abraham	Genesis 16, 20, 22	
Joseph	Genesis 39 - 41	
Saul	I Samuel 13:9-13	
David	I Samuel 24, 26 2 Samuel 11	
Daniel	Daniel 1, 3	
Peter	John 18:15-18 Acts 3:12,13	
Judas	John 13:21-30	
Jesus	Matthew 4:1-11	
Ananias and Sapphira	Acts 5:1-11	

• Have you had an experience that can best be described as a season of Internal Integrity testing?

• If you don't yet walk with a limp, is it because you have avoided wrestling with God, or is it simply that you have not reached this place?

• Do you think God ever schedules a Round Two in the wrestling match? What examples of this do you see in the life of David?

10.

Sometimes the skills we most need for public work are developed in obscurity. In fact, this seems to be more the norm than the exception. So people in the United States reaching this season are faced with a dilemma. Our educational systems seem bent on teaching people how to package themselves well, regardless of the contents of the package. Candidates become shallow; interviewers become suspicious.

And the problem is not isolated to the U.S. A young lady from South Africa commented that an acquaintance had landed an internship in a prestigious management-consulting firm. He had no clue as to what he was doing, but he very quickly learned that things were fine "as long as you gave the impression that you knew what was going on." This problem is then compounded by inflated expectations of career fast-tracking, less-than-30-year-old millionaires, and stars who are writing autobiographies in their early 20s. (One good movie does not character make.)

THE FAST TRACK

The Skills Building season in God's plan seems to run counter to the fast track. My observation is that it often takes the form of 10 to 15 years of unglamorous work. The day in, day out drudgery that, bit by bit, hones our skills is also part of God's plan. There are a number of implications of this season:

- Every job isn't a life-long career. When we feel led into a new career, we should consider why we are there. In one situation, I felt clearly that God had directed me to join a reputable firm. After about 18 months things did not look good. On the surface everything was rosy. But at a lower level I saw an organization that had been built on money, and not on values. After some time I asked God, "Why did you bring me here?" The reply was clear as a bell: "To learn what bad management is like." It's tough to learn the consequences of bad management when all you have experienced is positive leadership. Find out why God has asked you to do what you are doing.

- Marry yourself to God's long-term leading in your life, not to a career that looks good on paper. I have made numerous suicide moves in order to grow into the person God wants me to be, rather than stay in a rut to achieve the status or position others thought I should strive for. Will money automatically follow such decisions? That's the wrong question, and it betrays our bias toward money as the only valid measure of worth.

- Let God be your promoter. When you wrap your white knuckles around your own career advancement, you set yourself on a collision course with God. As the psalmist says, "For promotion and power come from nowhere on earth, but only from God. He promotes one and deposes another."[47] God's pace of promotion varies greatly by individual. Learn to follow his pattern for you.

- Settle your identity. If you gain your sense of self-worth mainly from your job, you are at risk. If you are settled in being an obedient child of the King, changing fortunes in your career will less likely shake you.

- When others seem bent on ruining your progress, you can respond as Joseph did. "You meant it for harm, but God meant it for good."

- Ask yourself the tough question: Who has rights over my career? The right to a good (looking) career and Convergence are sometimes diametrically opposed.

---

[47] Psalm 75:6-7, *Living Bible*

- Recognize the risks of shortcuts. Don't try to bust the cycle of skills building just so you can say, "I am on a fast track." Fast tracks to nowhere just get you nowhere quicker.

Convergence is often many little things we have done in our lives coming together to be woven into a fine, rich tapestry. It is not uncommon for us to spend 20, 30, 40 years winding those threads onto their spools before the author and finisher of our tapestry is ready to work them all together. Don't abandon the spools before they are filled appropriately. Quick isn't always better.

SERIAL CAREER TRACKER

Young people face a particularly difficult challenge in the Skills Building season. The "good old days" of predictable careers are over. If there is no such thing as job security, how do I commit myself to long-term skills building? If no one else is making long-term plans for me, how do I plan? The uncertainties in today's job market make it essential to get a grip on this season. Add to this the changing nature of work as we move from an asset-based to a knowledge-based global economy, and it is clear that we need fresh thinking about our careers.

I tease my father-in-law that he thinks I am a flake because I have worked for 4 companies in 20 years. He retired early after 40 years with Otis Elevators. Starting as an elevator mechanic, he rose to hold numerous senior executive positions around the world.

Even when I left high school, the choices were pretty clear. One year compulsory military service, four or five years of university, join the best firm in your field, and hop on the partner track. Today is different. Recently Lyn and I observed that Generation Y high-schoolers are embarking on careers as web designers and computer technicians while still at school. At the same time many of their counterparts in Generation X are leaving college with degrees but no clue about what they want to do. So how do you counter the uncertainties of career management in today's world? The answer lies in part in hearing God, and in gaining a long-term perspective on your life. In a sense, Convergence is about developing what we call life-management skills as opposed to career-management skills. Insecurity in the marketplace need not mean insecurity within.

LIFE IS WORK

Another point to consider here is one's definition of work. If we are to truly rest in a new definition of Career, we need to see Work as scripture sees it. Back in the first chapter of Genesis, God worked. It is there in black and white: "And on the seventh day God ended his work."[48]

God worked. Creation is his work. It reflects his identity, ability and will. It was subjected to self-assessment or scrutiny. The quality of the output was the measure of his work—"He saw that it was good"—and not the size of the paycheck or the acclaim from others.

We live in an age when people are either obsessed by work, or Utopian in their dreams of avoiding work, "maintenance" of everyday life, or both. But several things emerge from the accounts of God's work.

• Work is a pre-fall reality. Descriptions of paradise are normally work-free, but real life embraces real work.
• All of our work should reflect the character or nature of God in us.
• We should be content to judge the merit of our own work and not have our identity hinge on someone's decision about how much to pay us.

Elsewhere in scripture we see that receiving wages is fair and right.[49] The point here is that we should find our identity in Christ, not that we shouldn't earn an income. The enjoyment of work is a gift from God to everyone, not just "full-time ministers."

HONOR THOSE WHO HELP YOU BUILD YOUR SKILLS

There is a tendency among some in the western world to take for granted the individuals or organizations that invest themselves in our skills development. Instead of being grateful we find ourselves feeling,"My employer owes me a job, life owes me a living, they should invest in training me, they should pay me more, I should work shorter hours, I should get more vacation time, I want more of the profits, they should have less, they should mentor me, they should give me more stock options..."

[48] Genesis 2:2
[49] Luke 10:7

A friend once told me that his grandmother used to say, "If I could sell you for what you think you are worth and pay you what you are worth, I would be a millionaire." At some stage of our lives most of us seem to have inflated expectations. It can easily become the big corporation against us. But to get the most from our Skills Building season we must do three things:

• take ownership for our Skills Building.
• not think of ourselves more highly than we ought.[50]
• remember that God is our real master and it is a privilege to work for him.

The ability to grow our skills is at once a necessity and a privilege. Every once in a while go back to the Bible and examine the relationship between the apostles and their work.

> In the name of the Lord Jesus Christ, we command you, brother, to keep away from every brother who is idle and does not live according to the teaching you received from us. For you yourselves know how you ought to follow our example. We were not idle when we were with you, nor did we eat anyone's food without paying for it. On the contrary we worked night and day, laboring and toiling so that we would not be a burden to any of you...we gave you this rule: 'If a man will not work, he shall not eat.'[51]

Also look at the relationship between slaves and their masters.

> "All who are under the yoke of slavery should consider their masters worthy of full respect, so that God's name and our teaching may not be slandered."[52]

In the old days of trades and artisan apprenticeships, it was an honor to be trained by a skilled tradesman. In Silicon Valley some software developers will switch companies to work under a particularly gifted software engineer. In a Skills Building season we should honor those who are enhancing our skills. Their investment in us goes beyond what it costs them in time and money; they are imparting their values and vision. It is time they could have invested in others. Their investment helps ready us for the plans God has for us.

So go to work to worship God with your work, appreciative of those who make your worship possible.

---

[50] Romans 12:3
[51] 2 Thessalonians 3:6-10
[52] I Timothy 6:1

- Look back over your life. Have you ever walked away from a skills-building opportunity before it was completed? What, if anything, should you do about it?

- Who in scripture do you consider most like yourself; and what was their skills building phase?

- If you experience tension between your work and other aspects of life, is it rooted in your thinking about work? How much of your Career/Community tension is the result of fragmented thinking about work?

- If money were no issue, how would your work change?

- If you could add one skill to your life, what would it be?

- Does your sense of self-worth go up and down based on the size of your paycheck?

11.

CHOOSING YOUR SPOUSE

Not much serious writing is given to the choosing of your spouse. There's quite a bit on the do's and don'ts of dating—mostly the don'ts. But then, there's not much in the Bible either about choosing a wife or husband. I have concluded that this was one area where God got tired of taking the rap. After his provision of the perfect wife for Adam and Adam's admission that "she was good," God still ended up taking the heat. "The woman You gave me..." Now either Adam was little older than a teenager and was still in the mode of blaming his parents for even the best of things, or his newly found sinful nature was quick to blame others. Another factor is that in mankind's early history, marriages were generally arranged. So no need for great guidelines. "Son, this is your new wife." "Thanks, Dad." End of story.

Whatever the reason for scripture's minimal coverage of dating, the choosing of a husband or wife is one of our most life-shaping seasons. With Isaac and Rebecca, God was involved. Jacob's choice of Rachel was equally important. The story of Ruth and Boaz is more a woman's pursuit of the husband-to-be. Samson made some bad choices. David, some good, some bad. Solomon too many. Some were prophetic, some redemptive, and some just plain pathetic. Either way, our choice of a marriage partner makes a huge difference to our lives, positive or negative. Can God redeem bad marriage choices? Surely. Is it better to make a wise decision up-front? Of course.

One of the reasons that we make bad marriage choices is our own self-concept. Most of us grow up with some level of insecurity about ourselves. Too fat, too thin, too tall, too short. Too smart, too dumb, too pushy, too passive. In the stormy teenage years enough change is happening to our bodies, our brains and our beauty to leave the best of us feeling "not quite perfect." So we make a vow to ourselves that we will "show them" (whoever they are) that we really are quite cool and together and desirable by choosing the perfect marriage partner. Blonde, blue eyes, unlikely to gain weight in latter years, a head turning, traffic stopping, to-die-for beauty. For Barbie, there's always Ken. Tall, dark and handsome, sporting good pecs and (we even have a name for it) a "six pack" of abdomen muscles. (With a nice personality, of course. A little money wouldn't hurt either.)

Why do we have these fantasies? To look good. To feel better about ourselves. Twenty years later, if we haven't become a sad statistic at the nine-year average divorce mark, we are wondering why we are struggling to integrate our marriage and our Call. The big choice we made when we had more heat than light is coming back to haunt us.

SEASONS OF RELATIONSHIP

The "four stages of relationships" have been used to describe male-female relationships.

Forming	The honeymoon stage marked by flowers, candy, dates and humor.
Storming	Evidenced by idiosyncrasies, quirks, odd-isms and irritation. If it doesn't happen well in advance of marriage, leads to buyer's remorse.
Norming	The settling in stage where the rose-colored spectacles are crushed in the pathway, and optimism is replaced with realism.
Performing	The era when the relationship is less inwardly focused and begins to produce results that benefit others.

As helpful as these stages may be, they lack the essential pacing or regulation that a successful relationship needs.

The development of an effective relationship is much like the creation of a master painting. In our experience in counseling pre- and post-marriage couples, few have a good grasp of these concepts.

We once insisted that our daughter take a trip to South Africa with us to celebrate my mother's 70th birthday. With some reluctance she came. The way the flights worked, we had to return earlier and left Fay Maree with friends for an additional week. She called us from the Miami airport on the way home to California and excitedly told us that we had to talk when she returned. She had met a young man, and "It's a God thing." (As I mentioned earlier, God gets blamed for the most spurious of relational connections.) No big deal, except that Fay was all of 14, and the suitor a lofty 19. I was the original founder of FATBoys, Fathers Against Teenage Boys. Later Fay asked if the young man could come and spend a week with us. It was during that eventful week that Lyn and I sat them down and shared six important principles of relationship. The first one went something like this:

> Relationships are like painting a picture. You need three things, used in the correct sequence. First, there is the pencil of friendship," I said as I waved a pencil in front of them. "The broad outlines of the relationship are sketched out with a pencil. The boundaries are established, the price of making changes is low, and it involves some erasing and redoing.

> Second, is the black ink pen for adding detail and definiteness to the relationship. This is the season where you discover each others' spiritual gifts, and whether your giftings and passion for God are compatible.

> Finally comes the color. "Color is added when the physical relationship begins. Generally, there is little chance of going back and picking up the pencil again, or adding black ink details once the physical gets fired up."

We shared how many of the kids in their circle of friends began with the color. Big blotches of color dropped indiscriminately on the canvas. Then later they try to add definition by adding pencil to a scene already out of control. Few have any concept of how to discover and develop spiritual compatibility.

We then discussed the price tag of each item. A dollar for a pencil, $2 or $3 for an ink pen, and $12.50 for the paintbrush (fortunately the price tag was still on it). The price of a relationship that gets off on the wrong footing can be enormous. Years down the road, the real price can be that neither husband nor wife ever converge upon all God had in mind for them. They picked the wrong partner or have a series of abstract paintings clouding the picture.

Imagine painting a picture of a town. There's the:

> overall layout (your world view)
> the post office (how you communicate)
> the bank (what you feel about finances)
> the school-house (your thoughts on education)
> the church (your views on the church and philosophy of ministry)
> the hospital (health care, aging, value of life)
> the park (your thoughts on recreation)
> the movie theatre (what you feel about entertainment)
> the police station (how you think about law and order)
> the business center (your thoughts on career and making money)
> the town hall (your views on government, patriotism and nationality)

You get the picture. When we frame a relationship with physical involvement and we are on a course of commitment without understanding these fundamental things, we radically impair the likelihood of success.

The headlines of the remaining principles we discussed that day were as follows:
- Different commitments are appropriate at different times.
- Regulate, regulate, regulate. A particular danger with e-mail relationships is that people are prone to say much more than they would in person.
- Live each day (of the relationship) without making life-long decisions.
- Consider the short-term questions first: Do I want to get to know him/her? What are her/his personality traits? What experiences in my life does he/she need (and not need) to know? What are his/her views on the big areas of life (beyond the staring-me-in-the-face relational issues)?

- Learn to ask God questions first. Early in a relationship it is exciting and easy to talk. When problems arise we go to that person to get his/her counsel. But a time will come when God says, "When you have an issue, talk to me first." A big part of this is to ensure that we do not put our relationships with others ahead of him.

- Love God first and more. Matthew 6:33 says "Seek first the Kingdom of God and his righteousness..." Then comes everything else. The world's way is to scheme to get your own way, then ask for God's seal of approval. At this stage we harvest what we planted, and blessing is not a guaranteed result.

(RE)CHOOSING YOUR SPOUSE

"If I choose my wife correctly," asked the young intern, "can I avoid having to re-choose her later?" I laughed. "No way." What do we mean by re-choosing your wife or husband?

Let us begin with our own story. Lyn and I had begun praying and ministering together before we started dating. While we had seen each other around the small valley of Llandudno since we were seven years old, we hardly knew each other. Although once when I was young—I remember it clearly—I looked at her and wondered whether I would marry her one day.

Having said this, we hardly saw each other over the next 12 years. Occasionally we rode on a school bus together, once she wrote me a note and passed it on via a friend (her goals were no doubt evangelistic), and we attended a Scripture Union camp together one weekend when we were 16.

Around January of 1975 I had just completed my military service and attended a Youth for Christ youth group that Lyn and a friend had started in Hout Bay, a suburb of Cape Town. At the end of the evening I had (arrogantly) assessed the situation and said to Lyn, "What this youth group needs is some good leadership." Implied was, "And here I am." She thought she discerned some arrogance (but I was just functioning in my consulting gift, of course!).

By the time I came to really know Jesus around the time of my 19th birthday, I was very involved in the group and Lyn's leadership team. We began to spend time praying, leading and dialoguing together. Daily. We attended leadership training together, joined YFC's Associate Staff program, planned events, drove places together (with the normal 20-30 teenagers interwoven with us.) We wrote each other notes, shared things God was saying to us in our "quiet times" as they were called back then, and led meetings together.

I had my spiritual antennae up asking God whether this was someone with whom I should be having a more serious relationship. Nothing. I saw neither a red light nor a green light. I felt the freedom to build a friendship, but not to take the relationship any further.

The tricky part was that our relationship was growing. When you have so much time invested in each other, it would be odd for the emotional side to not develop.

I liked what I saw in Lyn. She was good with children, honored her parents, was a strong leader, had a well-balanced sense of God's grace, especially in areas where I would have been more performance-oriented and legalistic. She was also interesting. While to some she may have appeared to be a compliant "religious teenager," she had a strong sense of who she was. Lyn followed God in ways that less secure teens were unable to do.

Things were happening at two levels in my life. One was the emotional growth of a healthy relationship. Since I was car-less and Lyn had use of her mother's car, she occasionally drove me to the University of Cape Town. We planned youth meetings, shared perspectives on life, had opportunity to understand each others' dreams and passions. Both of us loved people. We were, as I recall, mostly willing to put the needs of others ahead of our own, and together we learned to hear God's voice about the small things.

Lyn's feelings for me were becoming obvious. (She'd be a lousy poker player.) Meanwhile both of us had separately told God that we did not want to enter into another flirtatious relationship. No more castles to conquer, no more mind or heart games. The next person we dated, we had to be willing to marry. We were the ripe old age of 19.

In early October of 1975 I was nearing the end of my first year at university and staying with a friend, Art Wouters, in his uncle's cottage. Art and his fianceé, Miranda, were having a few difficulties communicating. Being the third wheel in the party, I assumed the problem was me. I went outside to pray about it. As I was praying I thought, Why am I worrying about this? This is God's problem, not mine. Just then God spoke to me saying that I was trying to manage my own relationships. I had been in control, and usually the results weren't good. So I repented and surrendered my relationships to God, one by one. At the end of the prayer, my relationship with Lynelle Moller came to mind, and I said, "...and also my relationship with Lyn." It wasn't uppermost in my mind. This was a life transaction with God, not a discussion about Lyn.

So as we spent time together I observed this quality person in numerous settings. I watched her teach Sunday School, observed the way she related to her family, looked at the decisions she made about where to invest her time. Subconsciously, I was weighing whether this was God's woman for me.

Figuring out God's desires in a situation is often a progressive unfolding. When I was a kid I spent hours with my brother and cousins in Llandudno scratching in the dirt and making mud roads for our toy cars. When we'd pour the water on the sand, rivers would begin to flow. We'd channel them with our chubby hands, move stones out of the way, guide them this way then that way. We laid out a course for the water, but seldom saw it obediently follow our plan. So we constantly had to adapt. God has the same opportunity. Sure he knows everything, can control everything, and could do whatever he feels like. But often he gives us a nudge, we dig a channel, he pours the life-water of his Spirit... and we decide a rock would look good in the stream. Or the flow would be prettier if we had a few tributaries. Or what if we tried to get the water to flow uphill for a short distance. There is a perpetual planning and adapting process.

The next Sunday, October 5th 1975, Lynelle and I went for a stroll in Hout Bay. It turned out to be an historic walk for us both. Before housing development ate away at one of the last functioning dune systems in the Western Cape, there were large sand dunes in Hout Bay. We climbed one of the steepest dunes that overlooked the lower Disa River and Hout Bay Beach. Our conversation soon drifted to a series of letters we'd written each other in the preceding week or two.

As we perched above Hout Bay that Sunday afternoon we began to unpack those letters. Somehow I managed to get Lyn to fully explain her letters to me and 'fess-up that she loved me before I told her that I loved her too. I know it's not very manly. It was pretty sneaky, but there we are.

That Sunday night she went off to church and I stayed home to study. I was over the moon. Much of my delight was in the new start of a new relationship in a new way—I was love-struck, and pleased that I had not followed the pattern of past relationships. The other was that I was beginning to get some handle on the pattern by which God was speaking to me. As a new follower of Jesus, this was exciting. After years of knowing about the almighty, incredible God, about his Word, about his dealings in history, he was dealing with me, he was speaking to me, he was leading me along a path. After years of seeing through a fog, I was beginning to see more clearly. I was beginning to catch on. How incredibly exciting!

So from the early stages of our relationship we have done things together, and, hopefully, together with God. When we came to the United States we took a break from any formal role in ministry. The previous five years of pastoring while working at Price Waterhouse had left us in need of a rest. We decided on a one-year sabbatical. The one year became six, and the highway we traveled together in earlier years became two separate, parallel roads. During this season much happened in our lives separately: skills building, addition of gifts, some real desert experiences, internal integrity...each of us was growing. We were not growing apart. But there was enough space for us to grow separately. This did not create a problem. Putting it back together again...the re-integration of ourselves, this was the challenge.

RE-CHOOSE OR CRISIS

For the many valid seasons of our life, the devil has a counterfeit. Nowhere is this more evident than in the so-called mid-life crisis. There are jokes about it, movies inspired by it, car advertisements suggesting its cure, and millions of men to attest that it happened to them. So we assume every man will have a mid-life crisis, and it's nothing that a sports car won't solve. But there is an alternative.

One of God's antidotes to a crisis is re-choosing your spouse. You may counter, "That's fine for men, but women don't have mid-life crises." I beg to differ. The symptoms may be different, but the root is the same.

Around the ripe young age of 40 there is an attack on our identity which, if responded to correctly, can press us closer to God. We should graciously accept this rite of passage into a season that should find us basking in new abilities, maturity and limitations. It's all part of God's master plan of how we relate to him, others, and his world.

Unfortunately we have bought the media-myth that we don't need to age. Worse, we have believed that it is wrong to age. Younger is better. Firm forever, flabby never. Now, I have no argument with physical fitness. I am heart-broken, however, to see godly people fail to step through the door into the next season of their lives because they think they can be "forever young."

In the first letter of John he writes to three groups of people: children, young men, fathers. The Church today desperately lacks "fathers" because Church leaders and others cling to the mist of youth rather than own their age, and do not mature to a new season of effectiveness. I said to a church leader once that I sensed that God was taking him into the next season of his life; he was becoming an old man. My guess is he denied it, but when I see him from time to time, I look and think, "You are becoming an old man." Like it or not, there are passages and seasons. Like this leader we can deny it, refuse to change our management style, fail to recognize that the focus of our authority has shifted, and fail to pass on new things to young men and children. Or we can embrace the season, and extract all of its lessons.

A key part of this season is rediscovering your spouse. My assumption is that you and your spouse have both grown as people since you were married. With this growth comes new gifts, a greater ability to hear God, a new understanding of who God is. The Jesus you were following 20 years ago is the same, but you know and experience him in a different way. So God gives you an opportunity—I think an imperative—to rediscover and then re-choose your spouse. This is the true antidote for the mid-life crisis. Just as the insecurities about ourselves as teenagers are designed to press us into God where we discover our true identity, so our insecurities as 40-somethings are crafted to drive us closer, in Christ, to our mate.

An alternate explanation for the mid-life crisis is equally compelling: Os Guinness contends that it is the result of making early career choices inconsistent with our Call. By the time we get to 40, the dichotomy has worn us out.

SALAD TONGS

While attending a Business 2000 seminar at University of the Nations in Hawaii in 1995, Lyn and I received several clear messages of the need for us to re-integrate. As a team of people prayed for the delegates, someone had a mental image of us as silver salad tongs. Not the separate fork and spoon joined at the centers by a rivet or screw, but a single piece of silver, separate yet connected, moving vast quantities of fresh green salad.

The next picture was that of a stallion (evidently me) and a rider (the Holy Spirit) and Lyn as the bit and bridle.

Finally as a friend drove us to the airport that evening, he shared his image of a road that had been together, separated for a season and run in parallel, then joined together again. And the overall word for us was *integration*. We have spent much time since then struggling through the implications of that message to us.

Men and women sometimes shy away from rediscovering each other for fear of getting smothered. He has been busy career-building; she has built a family, a career, a home... and all without much help, thank you very much. Now, suddenly, he needs her. He is aware of his vulnerabilities and feels a stirring to draw closer to his family. She runs the car pool, the social life, the checkbook and the household. Everything is ticking over nicely, and she is not wild about his advances to "integrate." At our home we sometimes call it "tonging." After so many years developing their own identities and functions, it is tough for a husband and wife to hear a call to subject themselves to each other.

From our own experience, we know this is tough. Neither of us is high on the meek/submissive scale. We love each other, we communicate well, we interact well around projects and ideas. We are proud of each other's accomplishments and progress. But when it comes to the business of Convergence, which is so tightly linked to our identities, it does not work unless we discover a new combined identity with each party having the assurance that they will be represented.

"I JUST SUPPORT JIMMY'S MINISTRY"

Over the years, the Church's teaching on submission has resulted in passivity in some women when it comes to discovering their ministries. The idea of a combined ministry as co-heirs of God's grace with their husbands doesn't register on their radar. Many couples are able to pray together, laugh together, love together, but integration goes beyond these things. Supporting your husband is wonderful, but it won't protect you from the midlife crisis. You need integration.

exercises

X IS IMPORTANT TO INTEGRATION

Take a few moments to work through the worksheet below. It contains a list of propositional statements that are designed to open up dialogue with your spouse. Each of you should separately list your scores for each item (1=Disagree, 5=Strongly Agree), then discuss them. The objective is to talk, not to get a good mark. (5 is not always the best answer.)

Proposition	Ranking	Comments
Trust is important to Integration.		
Personal wholeness is important to Integration.		
I cannot be Integrated and co-dependent.		
I must forego who I am to be Integrated.		
I cannot be Integrated if I do not believe I am equal.		
I cannot be Integrated and independent.		
I can achieve personal wholeness without Integration.		
I can achieve Integration without personal wholeness.		
I have to have an equal career (to my spouse's) to achieve Integration.		
I must have financial flexibility in order to pursue Integration.		
My level of personal security affects my ability to Integrate.		
My level of personal security affects my desire to Integrate.		
I need to be at peace with my past to achieve Integration.		
My spouse must be at peace with my past to achieve Integration.		

- When have you and your spouse felt most in unison?

- When have you done things together for others that have brought you closer together?

- Where is the greatest overlap in your spiritual gifts?

- What causes your stomach to knot when you think about integrating with your husband or wife? What do you think is at the root of this reaction?

HUSBANDS LIVE CONSIDERATELY WITH YOUR WIVES...

...so that your prayers will not be cut off or hindered.[53] Chauvinism is not a new disease. Christ came to challenge our presuppositions on many fronts. I know that until the day I die God will be tapping me on my shoulder and saying, "We need to chat about your thinking on _____." I can't name all the areas; indeed a detailed list would be a little depressing. But we men need to be reminded, according to Peter, to live considerately with our wives.

Before you men zone out with the, "This doesn't apply to me" trick, I am not implying that you are solely responsible for putting your wife in a cage. Society in many forms encourages wives to be little more than caged parakeets. Some of it is intentional; some of it is simply the result of sinful society going its own way, and perhaps some is of it is the woman's own making. Whether it was through the teaching of the church or the messages of the playground, there is no virtue in anyone, male or female, living a caged—i.e., less than full potential—existence. And this is precisely why Jesus came, "... to undo the works of the devil."

EXERCISE (FOR HUSBANDS ONLY)

- So how does your wife feel: "free as a bird"? Or "she's only a bird in a gilded cage"?

- Have your wife's wings been clipped in any way? If so, how?

- What does the scriptural challenge to "live considerately with your wife" have to do with your role in bringing her to new freedom?

---

[53] I Peter 3:7

EXERCISE (FOR WIVES ONLY)

• So how do you feel: "free as a bird"? Or "only a bird in a gilded cage"? And is your husband aware of your feelings?

• What is the thing you fear most about integration with your husband?

• What is the vision you have of an integrated function in society/the Body of Christ for you and your husband?

EXERCISE: REVISITING THE 10-FS

• Go through the 10-F exercise and view/mark how you think your spouse feels about each F. How much margin does s/he think s/he has? (refer to p.7)

• Now map your scores and your spouse's scores on the spider chart below.

• This example of a 10-F Gap Map is included as an illustration. (This is not the assessment for anyone mentioned in these materials.)

• Discuss the differences and similarities with your spouse. What opportunities for a better understanding of each other emerge from this exercise?

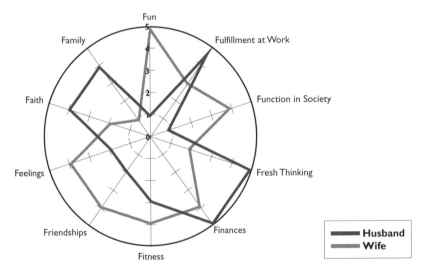

12.

There is no avoiding the desert.

God has an infinite number of ways to shape us into people who come to a point of Convergence, so the desert will look a little different to each of us. But the lessons are universal.

Are there those who oppose my views? Surely. A friend e-mailed to say that his time in the desert was not "alone with God" as I had predicted, but simply "alone." A waste of two years. Perhaps the Aarons, Jonahs and modern-day melancholics would agree with him. Certainly a whole generation of Israelites who left Egypt and fell short of Canaan might see the desert as a waste. But the fruit of the desert was a nation of Promised Land-owners.

Many have navigated the desert gracefully. We have peeped at Abraham, Jacob, Joseph, Moses and David. Let's turn to some others and examine their story.

NEBUCHADNEZZAR AND FRIENDS

By all accounts he was a big cheese. He ruled nations, had a dynasty that stretched for thousands of miles, had coffers full of the finest, and people bowing and scraping left and right. Then he got cocky and made the mistake of thinking that somehow his own hand had achieved it all. A party, a prophet's appearance, and pretty soon he's chewing grass like your garden-variety cow. For seven years.

Then there's Saul. Fancy education in the best academic circles, on a career fast track, legendary among the elite. Then God gets hold of him. Now, had we written the script, he would have been giving his testimony at the Christian business breakfast the following week. Instead this brilliant mind seemed to drop off the radar for about 15 years.

Nehemiah's desert was palatial. But it was still a desert. Serving as an exile in the courts of a foreign king, sipping non-kosher wine to see if it was laced was not the career goal of a good Jewish boy from Jerusalem. But for years and years he did it.

Let's take a closer look at the desert season. Consider your own life and mark the points of identification that you have with those listed below. These items are not academic. All of them come from my own desert season which was as glorious as it was painful. Many positive things happened in my parallel seasons of Skills Building and Internal Integrity. God's medicine often comes with a glass of fresh water.

WHY DO WE NEED THE DESERT?

That's a fair question: Why do we need the desert? Surely when we became followers of Jesus, we became "a new creation; the old has gone, the new has come!"[54]

Not so fast. A preacher once told his congregation that as long as he was their pastor, they would not get out of Romans chapter 7. Romans 8 is full of life-in-the-Spirit things; Romans 7 is quite clear about our sinful nature. "I know that nothing good lives in me, that is, in my sinful nature. For I have the desire to do what is good, but cannot carry it out."[55]

I remember preaching on this verse once and an elderly, straightforward Dutch lady in the congregation raised her hand and asked, "Do you really believe dat in you is no good ting?" "Yes", I replied. "Then you are a bloody liar!" said she. Sometimes even others (except our mothers) find it hard to believe that in us "is no good thing." Why?

---

[54] 2 Corinthians 5:17
[55] Romans 7:18

In the early days of our relationship with God it seems he does some interior decorating. New paint, fresh wardrobe, air freshener, quit smoking, stripped wallpaper, cleaning up our reading habits, clean windows, less TV, etc., etc.. By the end of the first six months we think we have been through the ringer and, looking pretty scrubbed up, we secretly wonder, Is there anything left to change?

Then comes the structural work. Drainage, finding the source of subterranean rot, re-wiring, taking apart and healing the stimulus and response system, foundation repair, tackling the skewed walls of our personalities at their source: bad foundations. And while some of this work goes on, the house can be unlivable. When God jacks up your house to recast the foundations, it's hard to keep going with religion-as-usual. When he strips you down to the studs, don't try to wallpaper. When he takes off your roof to tackle the leakage, the rot and the heat loss, you're better off in the desert.

Why do we need the desert? Because we need to become more like Jesus. And the everyday clutter of life usually anaesthetizes us to our need for fundamental fixing.

What are the objectives of the desert?

> To make me more grounded in God
> and his grace
> so that in the future I may serve him
> more broadly,
> and more safely,
> and more deeply.

METHODS OF THE DESERT

God has an infinite number of ways to accomplish his purposes in us. He is more interested in our deep-down growth towards his likeness than he is in securing our comfort. These are some of the things that seem common to the desert experience:

- Loneliness
- Being misunderstood
- Minimal use of talents and spiritual gifts
- The frustration of seeing what ought to be done, but having no influence or invitation to do it
- Start-and-stop friendships (as would-be friends pass you by for association with those who are "more successful")
- Financial stretching, but never too far
- More time in the gospels than in the letters or Acts—more emphasis on being a follower than on doing great works or churchy accomplishments
- Uprooting[56]
- Spiritual insignificance—this often follows uprooting: remember, no one knows who you are and what you have accomplished in the past
- Pruning, to the stump
- A dislocated hip

...and, failing all else, the old foot-of-God-on-the-neck trick.

CHARACTERISTICS OF DESERT UNIVERSITY STUDENTS

It's easy to spot them on the campus of life. They often seem a bit drifty; when you talk you recognize that they are 'convinced that God brought me here... but I don't know why.' They seem to be coasting a bit, and the smart ones don't respond readily to appeals for action or subtle guilt trips. Frankly, they don't have the energy. Here are some of the symptoms of those with desert fever:

- Not enough spiritual energy to blow their nose
- Care free
- Few great "words from the Lord" for others
- Saying No more than Yes
- Freedom from needing man's approval
- More clues about five years from now than about tomorrow
- Watching God make things grow without busily slapping up their own scaffolding
- Significance derived from God in them, not God through them

[56] A number of people have expressed a pre-disposition against relocation, and they have questioned whether God wants one to move. Even a cursory review of the lives of many historical characters shows that God often uses relocation as a means of growth, expanding one's sphere of influence, broadening thinking and deepening dependence on him. Starting with Adam and Eve (out of the garden), to Noah (first in on-time departures: imagine a 120 year wait!), Abraham, Jacob (perhaps by his own doing, but probably by God's sovereignty), Joseph, Moses...the list goes on. Do not forget Jesus, most of the original apostles & Paul. The world of modern missions grew, at least to some extent, out of the Moravians, a people who had become accustomed to being on the move.

- Slowly unfolding vision
- Reticence to touch what emerges from the dust
- Walking with a stick

CHALLENGES OF THE DESERT

Given the choice, most of us would rather avoid the desert. We are afraid that it will last forever and we have plenty of suggestions for God about better ways to achieve the same results. Once we have experienced the desert for a while, we may be so comfortable that we decide to stay there. So there are challenges at the desert entrances and exits:

- Resisting going in
- Self-pity (for the melancholics)
- Withdrawal from things you should be connected to
- Attempting to stay connected to things from which you should be withdrawing
- A short term focus (Neglecting to ask, "How long, O Lord" up front)
- Maintaining basic spiritual disciplines when there's no audience to keep you on your toes
- Bugs creeping out from under rocks you thought were safe
- Waking up from the big yawn
- Becoming a crusty old cynic
- Resisting coming out

Like much of life, God's sovereignty seems to be the determinant of when we go in and when we come out of the desert. Elijah is a classic example.

> [1]Now Elijah the Tishbite, from Tishbe in Gilead, said to Ahab, "As the LORD, the God of Israel, lives, whom I serve, there will be neither dew nor rain in the next few years except at my word."

> [2]Then the word of the LORD came to Elijah: [3]"Leave here, turn eastward and hide in the Kerith Ravine, east of the Jordan. [4]You will drink from the brook, and I have ordered the ravens to feed you there." [5]So he did what the LORD had told him. He went to the Kerith Ravine, east of the Jordan, and stayed there. [6]The

ravens brought him bread and meat in the morning and bread and meat in the evening, and he drank from the brook.

[7]Some time later the brook dried up because there had been no rain in the land. [8]Then the word of the LORD came to him: [9]"Go at once to Zarephath of Sidon and stay there."[57]

PRIZES OF THE DESERT

Why submit to the desert? Perhaps the greatest reason is simply to be a Father pleaser. Obedience is one reason; the prizes of the desert, another. What are some of these prizes?

- Less concern about the little things that don't really add up to anything
- More God-centric and less spiritual-resume-centric (especially hard for clergy)
- More caution about who you entrust yourself to (especially those that don't have dust on their clothes)
- Deliverance from "charismatic-answeritis", the affliction of having to have God's "word" on everything at all times
- Being more organic than institutional (being more focused on real life than structure, on substance than form)
- More eagerness to know Jesus than to have answers about him.

Simply, Jesus.

The writer of Hebrews says:
"No discipline seems pleasant at the time, but painful. Later on, however, it produces a harvest of righteousness and peace for those who have been trained by it."

Enjoy the training. It is an essential piece of Convergence.

[57] I Kings 17:1-9

Look at the lives of the following characters and make one or two points about the person they were when they went into the desert, and what had changed when they came out.

Character	They went in...	They came out...
Abraham		
Jacob		
Joseph		
Moses		
David		
Job		
Nebuchadnezzar		
Jesus		
Paul		

- Look back on your experience and consider any periods that were marked by the signs of the desert listed above. Check off the symptoms you have experienced.

- Have there been times when you have resisted God's leading into the desert?

- Has God ever directed you into a period of more background or inward focus?

- Have you, perhaps, experienced a desert season, but thought it was bad, or worse, a punishment?

- If God were to want to enroll you in the University of the Desert, what would be your greatest obstacles to stepping up to the registration table?

NOT EVERY SPEED-BUMP IS A DESERT EXPERIENCE

It is important to recognize that not every automobile accident, not every consequence of our own stupidity or sin, and not every bout of influenza is our desert experience. Some might need to be cautious to not develop a "woe is me" desert complex. How God deals with you is, after all, his business.

All of the above points are drawn from my season in the desert. Outwardly, things looked just fine. And inwardly I was at peace. But if I had tried to break out of the season before God was done with his pruning and shaping and re-rooting, I would have short-changed myself. While in my desert, occasionally people would come to me and say things like, "You could be contributing so much more. Your ministry is needed." It was not always easy, but I managed to "Just say No" to the expectations of others during this season. I could do it because I sensed the season. And looking back, I have been able to serve those same people in ways that were not possible before. Staying private (versus going public too soon) has been for my benefit as well as theirs.

Don't fight the desert. Let it complete its work in you. "Wait patiently for the Lord. Wait patiently for him to act." I suspect that if we insist on making appearances while we are supposed to be in the desert, God will let us come out early. But we should beware; we'll simply have to go back later. Having said that, my own experience was that God used me powerfully in the lives of others very sporadically while I was in my desert season, as if to encourage me by saying, "My gifts have not left you."

When you put your "pedal to the metal" in the desert, you simply spin your wheels. When you spin your wheels, you sink deeper in the desert sand. When you sink into the desert sand, instead of roaming its recesses peaceably, you become frustrated and crusty. You can try to take a dune buggy with you into the desert, but God has a slew of creative ways to exhaust your gas supply. The desert requires patience and grace. The desert is done on God's terms.

As we saw in Elijah's story, God provides in the desert. So enjoy your desert season, and stay there "until the brook dries up."

A WORD TO THOSE WHO HAVE HAD PUBLIC MIN-ISTRIES PRIOR TO THE UNIVERSITY OF THE DESERT

Some of your biggest critics will be those for whom you previously filled some pastoral or spiritual leadership role. When our season of obvious public ministry was over for a while, even those who had encouraged us to take a sabbatical looked down their noses at our apparent "lack of ministering." There was more than one friendly interrogation session: But what are you doing now? Do you think that God is still using you? Don't you miss the ministry? You are so busy with other things! When are you going to get back on track?

Someone once told me that people with needs have no mercy on those who can meet their needs. Most likely, many of the people who asked these questions were more interested in what I could do for them (and now wasn't doing) than in me as a friend. The true friends who simply love us for who we are saw the same set of circumstances quite differently: It is wonderful that you have the time to spend with pre-believers. You are being such a positive influence among us.

Why these seemingly opposing views of the same set of circumstances? A review of scripture (and the life experiences of many I know) indicates that the desert season is often a bridge that transitions us from one sphere of ministry to another. To be personal, my spiritual authority had come from my role as the pastor of a local church. Yet I have known since the mid-1980's that my Call lies beyond the boundaries of a particular local church. This was not necessarily apparent to others until much later. (No doubt it is still not apparent to many.)

Now, in Convergence, my influence draws on my experience as a pastor, but it is not the primary root of my influence. I have a new sphere of ministry: it is a wonderful place of non-dichotomized work that integrates Career, Call, Creativity and Community. One would almost have to invent a word for it: vocupation (vocation and occupation), bissions (business and missions)...the list could go on. None do it justice, so we speak of integration and convergence. The point here is: you cannot easily flip-flop from one sphere of influence to another without some down time, re-tooling and good old-fashioned rest. When we feel we "just have to be ministering" it is a warning sign that the work of the desert has yet to run its course.

The fact that words like "clergy" and "laity" get thrown from pulpits like verbal hand grenades complicates this whole scenario. "First class, second class." Preachers beware. When we have inadvertently preached the Christian class structure, we understand our own season in the desert that much less. When a pastor asked me how I felt when I "left the ministry" to just do business. I replied, "I didn't leave the ministry."

The desert is the awkward in-between. And the best thing to do is to smile at your critics, and shut up and enjoy the desert. Pretty soon you'll be busier than you wanted to be and you will yearn for those long, warm evenings in the desert with Jesus.

13.

OUR RIGHTS

One of Lyn's grandmothers used to often say, "Stick up for your rights, Lynnie." And in the normal course of things, it seems reasonable advice. But Jesus. He came along and upset the normal course of things. As the One who made it all—who dreamed it up, who brought it all into being, who had a rightful place of preeminence—he took on the nature of a servant. He gave up his rights. Convergence has nothing to do with getting your just desserts. It has everything to do with obedience.

Song of Songs 2:15 is an interesting verse on relationships:

> Catch for us the foxes,
> the little foxes
> that ruin the vineyards,
> our vineyards that are in bloom.

Any venture has the potential of being thwarted in its initial stages. "Little foxes" rub against the blossoming vines and bump off the flowers so that the potential for a full harvest is frustrated. The same is true for the journey towards Convergence.

The little foxes	The potential implications
Wrong concepts of God	• Not expecting the best • Make decisions out of fear • Insecurity • Rebellion
Rights to your own Career	• Looking good, but not feeling fulfilled • A string of job choices that never lead to Convergence
Finding your identity in the wrong places	• Pursuing work, relationships, money, fame and other meaning-substitutes instead of pursuing obedience
Being hung up on significance	• Getting caught in the cult of the individual
Refusing to make graceful transitions	• Getting what you longed for, hanging on to it too tightly, then watching it wither on the vine because you refused to move "with the cloud"
Lacking the faith to move into a position where God can bless you	• Having a predictable income stream, a predictable upstream float, and being bored with it all • Financial shortfall
Avoiding key seasons	• Never being ready for Convergence.

THE LINE IN THE SAND

We don't mean to, but we do it. On one side stands the Almighty God, a few feet away we stand and face him. And between us we have drawn a line in the sand. "I was willing to give up smoking, I was willing to stop this, I was willing to start that, but please don't ask me to _____."

I was proud of myself. I was nearly 19 years old. Finally, I had come to a real relationship with Jesus, and I was doing well. Up at around 5:30 each morning. William Barclay commentaries, extensive note-taking. I remember thinking to myself, I don't think I am holding out on God in any area. I am pretty much squeaky clean. Except for one thing. I loved to dodge the traffic lights when driving down Loop Street (prophetically named) in downtown Cape Town. If you timed it just right, you could hit all of the lights from one end to the other as they changed from red to green. I was on my way to a Youth for Christ camp. It was my birthday. And I was pushing Sammy, my sister's 6Volt VW Beetle down Loop Street about as swiftly as I could. I glanced over my shoulder to change lanes, and when I looked back in front of me the pale blue Ford Escort was stopped dead in its tracks. Wham! Happy Birthday! I had run into my line in the sand, the one thing I wasn't ready to give to God.

The process of sanctification takes time. My arrogance made me feel I was near the end of the journey when I had hardly started. Now in some respects the "getting rid of sin" part of sanctification is easy. When the issue is no longer behavior, but Who's running the show? and Will I trust him?, then we can easily draw a subconscious line in the sand. Does God have a right to tell you where to live, what car to drive, what to name your child, where to work, whether to travel?

Take a close look at your index finger. See any dust there? Any dirt under the fingernail? Ask the Holy Spirit to let you know where you have drawn any lines in the sand (not if, but where.)

LAZINESS

A major obstacle to Convergence is laziness, particularly in a world where we confuse activity and work.

"One who is slack in his work is brother to one who destroys."[58]

Meetings, cell phones, crazy schedules all lull us into laziness in the midst of busyness. Convergence demands the focus to clear the decks of the divergent. Failure to muster the energy to unravel and make sense of the threads of life is a hindrance to Convergence. In addition, the absence of language, frameworks, markers and milestones will obstruct Convergence.

HOLES IN OUR WORLDVIEW

Our street, our suburb, our school, our social network. Wherever you are, you are local, and life has to be lived out at the local level. But our particular locality must be a springboard to a broader worldview. We

---

[58] Proverbs 18:9

must understand not just the people beyond our community, but the patterns, the trends and the meaning of the times at the national and international levels. This creates a grid against which we can examine our Call, our Career and our Creativity. Even community, for an increasing number of people, extends well beyond their immediate locale.

And worldview is not just about geography and location. I think that when Jesus returned from the trips with his disciples and stopped in for tea at Martha's vineyard, they probably chatted about what God was up to in the world and how they were a part of it. What on earth is God up to nowadays, and how can you get into his game? Good questions for those who want to get on the road to Convergence.

FAILURE TO WORK A LONG-RANGE PLAN

In the early 1990s I brainstormed with friends about developing plans to transition from 60-hour weeks to something that would free up time for more direct Kingdom purposes. We drew diagrams of stepping down time in one's occupation to pick up one's vocation. I once received e-mail from an old friend that read:

> Brett,
> While unpacking here in Kent, Ohio, I came across an old PFC [Professionals for Christ] newsletter. I read my first fund raising letter from '94 which said that I was starting a small consulting business that will eventually support me full time in ministry. I did not realize at the time how much God would use Add On Consulting. I merged my client base with another company this past year and I get a percentage of gross consulting hours paid monthly - (which goes farther in Ohio $). This has truly freed me up to do this Vineyard Church plant. The process has taken just about 5 years as you said it would. I have learned a lot as an entrepreneur that is transferable to pastoring. I know I have said thanks before, but I just wanted to say so again: Thank you for helping me the way you have.

Doug had a long-term plan. He took risks to achieve it, leaving a secure job as an in-house Information Technology professional to start his own business. At the outset we worked together on Professionals for Christ.

Within a year his startup had grown to the point where it could support him fully, and he moved on. But he never let go of his dream of fulfilling his call to pastor. His e-mail tells the story of how he did what many just dream about. Dreams are great, but they need legs to get you places. Doug's a man with dreams that grew legs. How are your dreams? And do they have legs yet?

WILLING TO DO

Before you can see it, sometimes you must be willing to do it. Sure we'll meet some folks who knew exactly what to do but they balked at God's possibilities. They are like a batter at the plate and God is throwing them lots of strikes. They stand over the plate twitching occasionally, but unwilling to take a swing. None of the balls has yet looked just perfect. They are like cricketers at the crease who watch the fast balls whiz by, but are afraid to play any strokes.

For many others the Call is not obvious because they are subconsciously unwilling to face the consequences of the Call. Their lives are filled with questions about Call: Could God be saying this? What if it is God? What if it isn't?

They have collected many ideas. If they are really talented, others have come to them with ideas.

What if you did this? If I gave you this money and that opportunity, you could...

Changing the analogy, they are like a potential homeowner standing over a table covered in architectural blueprints. Each one seems to be a wonderful plan. The longer they stand looking at the fine ideas, the more others try to help. Friends throw in plans, wives and husbands draw up plans, employers create plans, venture capitalists ask for plans, ministry leaders say, "God loves you and I have a plan for your life." Some of the plans come with strings attached. Others are plain good opportunities.

Over the years these people appear to grow more confused than ever. Less sure of themselves. Less confidant that they can build what's been presented to them. They say they don't know, but slowly a weight of evidence has been amassing. And God begins to craft situations to ready them for building, and for going with the plan that is his.

Maybe it's a career diversion that is really a season of skill building. Back to the table. Still they make no choice. Then comes an Internal Integrity test, and they return to the table a little more willing to do it God's way. Then there is a trip down a promising career track that, instead of success, delivers misunderstanding, being overlooked and even scorn. They come back to the table more leery of man's plans, and a tad more willing to ignore the glitzy game plan and go for the substantive steps of obedience.

God is quite patient. We can diddle and dawdle and claim we hear no call when the answer lies in plain view behind our fear. We have to ask ourselves, What do I fear?

- I won't be able to pull it off
- The Call will not look good enough to my friends
- I will have to give up a title
- My income may go down
- I will have to relocate
- It might not be the best thing for me, my family
- I don't know if I am worthy of such a call (Get over it. You are not.)

If we are still haunted by these types of questions, beware the University of the Desert. That desert has a way of weeding these things out of us.

On the other hand, you might genuinely want God's call, and you have experienced the Seven Seasons, yet you are still drowning in the cacophony of options. "Be still..." Consider what you have learned about who you are. Reflect on what you really value—what are your non-negotiables? Affirm again the few gifts that are you. (Separate these from the many things you could do if you had to.) "... and know that I am God." Remember what you have learned about God and his character. Brush the world's dust off the plate. Tune out the blare of the advertising on the stadium walls and the bright lights of seductive success or glamorous significance. Make a list of what you know about God and his dealings with you. Then take a swing at what comes your way.

If the sporting analogy leaves you frozen at the plate, go back to the drawing table. Reconsider the many plans you may have made. Reject those that simply make you look good; embrace those that resonate with a "deep calls to deep" quality. Assess where the weight of evidence is stacked. Your Call may be more obvious than you think.

If God is good, his call is good. No fear!

WHO AM I?

For some portion of the population there is the tough obstacle of not knowing who they are. Obstacle might be too definite a word, because you can easily see an obstacle. And not knowing who I am is a tough one for me to see. In my discussions with people over time, my ears have become attuned to the statements "I have always wanted to..." "I have always believed..." and "I have always known..." This is no scientific fact, but I have discovered it usually means, "I have recently discovered about myself..." or more pointedly, "I don't really know myself, but if I drive a few stakes in the ground (in the form of absolute statements) I will feel better about what I don't know." What has all this to do with Call and Convergence? If you don't know yourself, it is hard to know your call. And if you don't know your God, it is hard to know yourself. (If this sounds a bit like you, and you glossed over the first season—Faith and Knowing God—you might want to re-visit the essence of who God is. A distorted view of God leads to a distorted view of ourselves.)

If I don't know myself, then I place an unrealistic burden on others to (a) know me, and (b) clarify my call on my behalf. This book can help clarify what one does and does not know about Career, Call, Creativity and Community, but it may not do the job if you haven't done the hard work of facing up to who you are and are not.

THE TIME HAS NOT YET COME

The path to Convergence is usually clearer in retrospect. The same is true in the area of Call. Like Abraham, we may know where we've been called from before we know where we have been called to. More important, we may know who has called us better than why he called us. The area of Call is a mixture of mystery and certainty. Nonetheless our thinking can be aided if we are clear on what we know, and honest about what we don't yet know. This is especially true when we are more than likely some years away from Convergence. Not all factors hindering Convergence in our lives are controllable. Our job is to obey, resting in the fact that "my times are in His hands."

14.

It's fair to ask about the relevance of Convergence to children. On the one hand, kids have a long way to go before their direct influence over Convergence becomes apparent. On the other hand, many people don't achieve Convergence simply because they fail to develop right patterns of decision-making when they are young. For a host of reasons, I believe it is important for teenagers to at least understand the questions they should ask as they squeeze through their rites of passage within four or five flicks of the annual calendar.

Why is it that children need the thinking tools of Convergence?

- Information is available everywhere, but life-skills are hard to come by.
- World views are in flux.
- Career choices are hard to untangle.
- Their predecessor generations have been short on hope and answers.
- Today's children face different and more direct social challenges than previous generations.
- They need to be anchored in order to weather the serious changes the Church is undergoing today.

The foundation for Convergence begins early in life and uneven growth in the 10-Fs is much harder to counter in later years. We have seen the fruit of this in men who grew up without fathers and now lack basic life skills, teenagers wanting to leave home too soon, children returning to live with their parents at age 40, and people simply never growing up. (Add to this the eternal youth syndrome and the increased incidence of millionaires under 30, and we have the recipe for undirected or passionless living.)

A FRAMEWORK FOR THINKING ABOUT LIFE

In the late 1980s I began to create a model of personal planning that addressed the major components of my life. I soon became convinced that monthly planning using this model was one of the most spiritual exercises I conducted. So as not to create the impression that I'm one given to rigor and personal discipline, I'll confess the planning was more grace than grit. I did not convert each goal into an activity on my calendar. But somehow just having thought-through, documented goals was important.

The original model had five major areas.

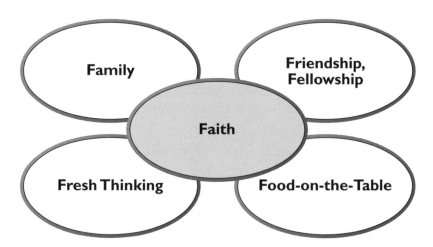

I spent a few minutes most weeks setting goals in each area. Food-on-the-table covered my work goals, Fresh Thinking was intended to keep me growing beyond my current mental models. The social side of life was covered by Friendship/Fellowship, and Family and Faith seemed to pick up the rest. It wasn't perfect, but it provided a framework.

Then in 1995, Lyn and I began to teach on the concept of *Margin*. The underlying reason was simple: if we didn't make space for God to do the uncommon in our lives, it might never happen. The alternative to this truism seems to be that God has to use a catastrophe, and we hoped to avoid that scenario. The series of presentations we developed for various e-Quip meetings expanded to include the 10-F Model and the 10-F Gap Map.

In 1997, The Institute began working with Prison Fellowship Ministries to develop a program that would minister to children of prisoners on a year round basis. Dubbed "The Angel Tree Network" because it builds on the hugely successful Angel Tree program, the model needed a way to understand the needs of a child. So we adapted the 10-F Model and tested its application to children.[59]

IT TAKES A NETWORK

The number and frequency of inputs into the lives of our children is exploding and becoming difficult to control. Billboards, newscasts, magazines, e-mails, pagers with secret codes, telephones, cell phones, wristwatch beepers, chat rooms, teen-targeted web sites, push-advertising on the generic web browsers, smart pets, video games, internet gaming... and lest we forget, the old nemesis, TV. Yikes! Add to this the tendency of teenagers to go overboard on something until they are sick of it... then drop it, and we have an input management crisis. How can we counterbalance the onslaught of this megaphony of other inputs? In our experience, it takes a network to impact a child.

The Institute has developed the concept of an Impact Network.[60] In its work with both non-profit and business organizations, we help design and develop a network (or collection of people and organizations) unique to each organization that will help it achieve some desired future Impact.

---

[59] We have given permission to Prison Fellowship Ministries to use the 10-F Model as the basis for their Angel Tree Network program aimed at the children of prisoners and their families. The model is also being used by The Institute for Innovation, Integration & Impact for its staff planning and personnel development.
[60] The Impact Network is part of the The I⁴ Methodology © I⁴ International—Used with permission.

By combining the network concept and the 10-F model, we have the framework for placing children on a path to Convergence from an early age.

The 10-F model recognizes that a variety of organizations are engaged in bringing things into the life of a person. TV, movies, school, sports figures, doctors, ... There are numerous contributors at each point of influence, namely, for each of the 10-Fs. The subconscious role of the parents is that of network manager. Mothers seem best equipped for this task with an innate ability to juggle multiple balls, manage conflicts, and create the right alchemy of ingredients to benefit and nurture a child.

The 10-F model is designed to help caregivers identify needs for input into the lives of children and adults, and then tap into good sources of such nurture and growth. It aims to move the business of raising responsible people from an unconscious to a conscious competency.

IN THE BEGINNING... WAS A NETWORK

The network is not a new concept. It can easily be argued that the concept of both the 10-Fs and the network is inherent in who God is—the Trinity. God is a god who communicates, relates and functions cooperatively. Further, he places us in communities because that is where we get to know him best. The early Hebrews practiced community in many ways. Family rituals, life at the synagogue, special celebrations, formalized instruction, personal relationships. All were part and parcel of their being. In very natural ways, the whole community contributed to the raising of the children. And at the center of much of Jewish activity was the mother. In many respects she was the 'network manager' in that she oversaw the influences that shaped the identity of her most precious possessions, her children.

RE-SHAPING THE NETWORK

The rate of change in society is phenomenal. Due to the reach of the Internet and other media, the increased flow of information and ideas is incredible. With this comes the entrance of new influences on our 10-Fs on a daily basis. On top of this, we are growing and changing. The net result is that we have to re-arrange the ingredients in our network frequently, but particularly as we transition from children to teenagers to young adults to adults. In the table below, consider two questions: Who is managing the network? Who are the players in the network? Note how things change as the child gets older in the two examples of Family and Faith.

Network Management 10-F Area	1-6 years of age: Mother-managed network	7-12 years Strong parental influence; limited child choices	13 - 18 years Self-managed network with parental 'exception management'
Family	Family-centered activities	Child-event centered (sports, school, church)	Peer-centered
Faith	Home Sunday School	Sunday School	Youth group, Young Life

The traditional role of the family in the child's network has been challenged for some time.

> The future battle over our minds is a battle for the individual soul, the individual personality as perceived by itself, 'What am I like? Who am I? Where [the family] used to reign supreme, today it faces competition; in the future, this competition will be even stiffer. A 1997 survey asked American MBA students what things they considered most important in life. Heading the list was building a career (75%), but the family ran a very close second (71 percent). Responses from these young Americans reveal the increased competition; if they stick to the ideals of their youth, these students will be facing a lifelong, daily challenge: job or family.[61]

In June of 1999 the National Marriage Project at Rutgers University released *The State of our Unions— The Social Health of Marriage in America*.[62] The statistics may not surprise us:

---

[61] *The Dream Society*, ibid

[62] David Popenoe and Barbara Whitehead, *The State of our Unions: The Social Health of Marriage in America* — http://marriage.rutgers.edu

- Since 1970 there has been a decline of one-third on the annual number of marriages per 1,000 women.
- The percentage of "very happy" marriages has decreased; after ten years only 25% of first marriages are successful (i.e., intact and reportedly happy)
- The percentage of children in single-parent homes has risen from nine percent in 1960 to 28% in 1998. Thirty-five percent of children now live apart from their biological fathers.

What is surprising, perhaps, is that against this backdrop of terrible statistics, the teenagers are hoping, or perhaps clutching, for something better. 83.1% of teenage girls say that having a good marriage and family life is "extremely important" (up from 80.2 percent in 1980.) The report goes on to say:

> Nonetheless, there are some reasons for hope. For example, given the increased importance of marriage to teenagers, it is possible that this generation will work hard at staying happily married. The decline in the unwed birth rate is also a good sign. And there are stirrings of a larger grass-roots marriage movement. Churches in more than a hundred communities have joined together to establish a common set of premarital counseling standards and practices for engaged couples.

This hopefulness suggests a window of opportunity for adults to play a role in shaping the values and strengthening the dreams of teenagers. It also underscores the importance of deliberately building the right network to support today's children.

Consider the lives of children in each major phase of development. Who are the partners you would choose to have in your child's network?

F Area	Child	Pre-Teen	Teenager
Fun			
Fulfillment at Work			
Function in Society			
Fresh Thinking			
Finances			
Fitness			
Friendships			
Feelings			
Faith			
Family			

THERE'S MANY A SLIP

"It's a holding ministry."

About 500 children passed through our hands over the 10 years that we led the youth group in Hout Bay, South Africa. After we had driven the last of the children home after youth group on a Saturday night, we often said to each other, "It's a holding ministry." Many late nights, many years of planning, praying and counseling; not always much to show for it. The risky areas seemed to be the passages. Not the hallways, but the passages from pre-teen to teen when they had outgrown Sunday School but not yet connected with a youth program. And the passage from teenager to adult, when they went to the army, university or their first job, and lost touch with their previous support network. There's many a slip in the passages of life.

What's worse, today the passages are becoming less predictable, and more slippery. Columnist Dave Barry's statement may be more than a humorous statement: "What I look forward to is continued immaturity followed by death." Pre-adolescents are maturing at odd ages. Teenagers are assaulted with adult stuff. Young adults think they're still teenagers. The baton gets dropped at the hand-offs precisely because we don't see the hand-offs coming. Age-appropriate, regulated, transitioned growth is rare.

All of these changes are leading some to predict that the standard age categories are going to be redefined. "Teenagers" are a creation of the second half of this century; they may disappear as a market or societal segment as teenagers become part of a new group called... "screenagers." These are the emerging product of the Internet era who are defining their life-maps using a set of inputs that none of their preceding generations had.

The 10-F model (with a long-term eye on Convergence) can help to secure the hand-offs by providing an understandable framework for all ages.

"INCREASING THE DENSITY OF RESPONSIBLE ADULTS"

When we came to the United States I realized how much we missed the support structure we'd enjoyed in South Africa. We'd been busy there: a full-time job at Price Waterhouse and a full-time job leading a local church. There were elders' meetings several times a week, sermons to prepare, clients to audit and consult, people to counsel, administration to perform, worship to lead, friends to reach out to. But there was also an organic network of support. People to cook meals, watch our children, trim trees, fix cars, plan vacations, guide our children, pray for us, counsel us in many areas, support our (very young) leadership. Without that network in the U.S., as a father I had to dedicate much more time to the day-to-day routine of my family.

Today we make a conscious effort to expose our children to the company, thinking, prayer and worldview of godly people. When friends sleep over, they ask our kids questions. We try to give them time alone together so that they can talk about stuff that is not easy to broach with Mom and Dad. They laugh with each other, get mad at each other, cry with each other, and love each other. We also send our children away to stay with others when possible. They relate differently to each other when we are not around hogging the conversation. We spend money on going places and having others come to us. We nurture the network.

John Dilulio and other researchers claim that disadvantaged children are most helped by "increasing the density of responsible adults" in their lives. The same holds true for "regular kids." As they go through their teenage years, other adults will be key to your children's finding themselves. Don't let the network happen by accident; actively build your child's Impact Network.

Complete a 10-F Assessment on your children. Now list the dominant influence in each of the F categories. (If you're a pre-adult reading this, go ahead and do it for yourself. If your parents are with you, compare results and talk about your differences in scores.)

F Area	Score (1 - 5)	Dominant Influence
Fun		
Fulfillment at Work		
Function in Society		
Fresh Thinking		
Finances		
Fitness		
Friendships		
Feelings		
Faith		
Family		

LIFE MANAGEMENT SKILLS

What will the next century feel like for our children? What are the one or two big decisions they will have to face in regard to their Call, Community, Creativity and Career? And who is equipping your children to make the big decisions that come along? They will live in a world where there is a confluence of previously separate streams. Here are some examples:

- communications, content and computing
- nations and economies
- language barriers
- time boundaries
- barriers between people and technology (due to miniaturization and ubiquitous technologies)
- cultural barriers as the MTV generations look and sound quite similar around the world (America is exporting culture)

But will our children find Convergence in the area that matters the most? Will we overcome the fragmentation and model a new way of living out our faith? Or will the flaws of our own faulty foundations leave gaps in the walls of our lives?

WHAT CAN BE DONE TO PREPARE THEM FOR THE FUTURE?

In the old days, kids knew what their parents did for a living. Butcher, baker, candlestick maker. Farmer, doctor, engineer, teacher. They could see what mom and dad actually did. Today we are lucky if our children know the name of our company, let alone the industry we are in. If they don't know what we do, it is no surprise that they have few clues as to what they want to do when they grow up.

So how do we balance these seeming conflicts when:

- we recognize that our children are maturing earlier than we did
- we understand that they have little clue about the uncertain future
- the statistics say that children are getting older, but not maturing; in fact, many are returning home as older children at 35 and 40 years of age
- technology skills are developing at a pace that can outstrip character development

First, parents need to become their children's network managers and take steps to understand what that network should look like.

Second, we have to teach them the nitty-gritty process of figuring out what God wants on a daily basis. Our experience thus far is this: involve them in decisions, seek their counsel, expect them to hear God on behalf of the family.

Our children have been the instigators in a few big property decisions. Fay got chatting to an elderly man outside his house one day; she was six years old. He complained about taxes, government and living in California. He said he wanted to live in Oregon. We bought his house without it even going on the market.

Eight years later we needed to rent a larger house. We checked the rental listings and discovered four houses in a forty-mile stretch that met our criteria. We prayed and Lyn felt the kids would lead us to the next house. A few days later they came home and said some kids were leaving town and their rental was coming available. It didn't go on the market either and within a short period we moved in. We have come to expect that sometimes the only guidance we will get is going to be from our children.

Third, try to model integrated living for them. Sure, they may still want to break out of the mold and do their own thing. They may want to live a fragmented life for a while. But they will have been ruined for the ordinary if they have seen you model the components of life in an integrated whole.

Fourth, teach them to ask the right questions. In the planning supplement to this book[63] there are some tools that help in asking the right questions. Consider how these may apply to your children.

Fifth, take deliberate steps to instill your values in your children. In the normal course of events, they will take on your values just through being with you. But don't rest on your laurels. Deliberately ask questions and make observations about their values.

Finally, seriously evaluate whether the mad dash to college is right for your child. Our observations over 25-plus years is that many teenagers

[63] For supplemental materials, see www.convergencebook.com

need a break after high school before they dive headlong into college. We are not talking about a party break, but a bookmark in the routine of study. We recommend that this be considered for a series of reasons:

- High school does not always do a great job of preparing students for college. Junior colleges have become finishing colleges, completing the work that high schools would have done in the not-too-distant past.

- Parents are not finished preparing their children for their role in the world. While at high school, the bearers of the Holy Grail are twenty-something year old teachers. Your children are turning to them for answers sometimes in a way that closes them to hearing from you. So many kids leave high school without having basic life skills. Yet these same children start at age 14 talking about how they can't wait to get their own apartment and do their own thing. Their fixation with leaving (and the American parents' desire to get them out of the nest quickly) can easily have the opposite of the desired effect. The goal is for them to grow up; the result is that the last season in the cocoon which is designed to bring them strength, is short-circuited. Instead of growing them up, they are ill-prepared for adult responsibilities.

- Many children are growing up too quickly physically and socially, without the character, emotional and spiritual development to complement this early development. The onslaught of media and training we provide to warn them of various ills means we have to expose our children to things earlier than we would like. There is some premature loss of innocence. But some things cannot be rushed, and often we are too quick to push our children into the world half-armed to fight the battles they will face.

- Many children are shielded from service opportunities. Society places great virtue in establishing a regimen of school, sports, arts, dance, karate, music and more. We are dizzied by our children's activities. And all of this can leave little time for them to learn how to serve others. Even in church, they have programs tailored to them and youth ministers hired to serve them, and they are not asked to consistently serve others.

You might have guessed that some of this comes out of our own experience. In the churches we attended as youth, one began teaching three- and four-year-olds as a teenager. You were conscripted and trained to be part of the staff—unpaid, of course. At about 16, Lyn started a youth group in her home. For years, many of the young people who attended were older than she was. Service was expected.

When boys left high school—it was okay to call them boys then—they generally spent a year or two in compulsory military training before going to college. Compulsory military training draws on a cross-section of society. We were forced to bungalow with people we didn't even know existed. We were taken outside of our cultural comfort zone, physically, socially and mentally. I noticed a huge difference between the level of maturity of those who went to college directly from school, and those who did their military stint first. Some people wasted that time and did unsavory things. Most boys just grew up. Was the army good for everyone? No. Could everyone "be all that they could be"? Not at all. But the notion of serving people you didn't want to serve and doing things you didn't want to do, all for three bucks a day, had some merit.

I am not advocating that we send our kids off to the military. (Given the choice, I would have avoided it.) I am suggesting that they volunteer a year of their time between high school and college and enter a formal program where they can be discipled, equipped and taken into service opportunities, preferably in other nations.

This won't guarantee Convergence at a later stage; but it will help stretch their worldview beyond the narrow confines of their high school or college campus. It will fire their imagination for what God is doing in the world. It will provide a channel for their gifts to the needy. It will heighten their awareness of their own privileged position on this planet. It will underscore the reason for later academic training. These things may help them lessen the struggle with Convergence when they are older.

exercises

LOOKING AT FAMILY CONTENTMENT

• Complete the 10-F data and chart for each member of your family.

• Discuss the outcomes as a family.

THE 10-F ASSESSMENT

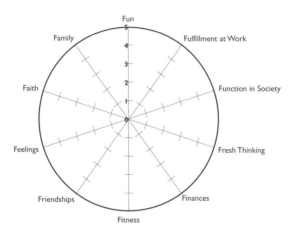

	Husband	**Wife**	**Child**
Fun			
Fulfillment at Work			
Function in Society			
Fresh Thinking			
Finances			
Fitness			
Friendships			
Feelings			
Faith			
Family			

• This chart will help you understand where you are today, and where you might need to make adjustments so that God can do His full work in you and your family.

15.

People remember stories. They forget whole speeches, but remember the stories. They forget facts and figures, but can recall minute details of stories. From children to juveniles in prison to old people, we like hearing stories.

And each of us has a story. Not all of us understand the importance of telling it. Yet if we can tell our past we can tackle our future. Often when I meet someone I ask: "Tell me your story." This simple phrase opens up a slew of history. The telling of one's story builds a bridge. When getting to know someone, I want to fill in the missing pieces of the jigsaw. Where did they live, what school did they go to, what were the formative experiences in their lives.

We are living in an era where those in affluent countries are increasingly purchasing with their hearts. We are no longer buying just goods and services, but we are purchasing a piece of the story that is embedded in the products.

STORY-TELLING TOOLS

I recently sat down for dinner with my cousin and some friends in Atlanta. After we had been together for an hour or so I turned to my cousin and asked her, "So how are you doing?"

"What do you want to know?" she retorted. So I said I wanted to ask her about 10 areas. Beginning with her Faith, we walked through the 10-F model. Within about 20 minutes I had a good idea of how she was in all the important areas of her life. So I asked a waiter for a pen and a clean napkin and mapped out a radar or spider chart of her feelings about where she was in life. Next I suggested that she compare herself to her husband and talk about their similarities and differences. By the end of the evening we had created their 10-F Gap Map (see chapter 2) and had a meaningful dialogue with them and others at the table. The 10-F map can be a starting point for your story. Alternately, ask someone to tell you their story in each category.

Another way to tell your story is using the Seven Seasons. Take a while to consider whether you have experienced these or other seasons. How have they overlapped? What indicated the start and end of a season? When have you avoided seasons, or what do you wish you could have done quicker or slower? Why?

Alternately, choose some objects from your everyday life that are symbolic of your story. A teacup, a paintbrush, a vacuum cleaner, a vase, a baseball mitt. What were the dominant objects in different seasons? What things were consistent across all seasons? How do they help tell your story?

Now think through the things that are "common to man." Then take symbols of these things and lay them out on a piece of paper to depict your own epic. Hills, valleys, rain, sunshine, storm clouds, thunder, mist, spring, winter... Tell your story to someone using these earth-related symbols.

Or how about music: what music best described the different eras in your life? Was God there in the music? Could he have been?

DANGERS OF TELLING YOUR STORY

Revisionism: Re-writing the past to make it sound better than it was. "This is a true story; only the facts have been changed to protect the guilty."

The blame game: "My mother made me do it." While there may be truth to some of this, the purpose of telling your story is to understand how God has led you, what seasons you have been through, not to apportion blame for what you didn't do.

Covering the trail: Not every story is logical or pretty. In fact, many people fail to reach Convergence because they lacked the tools to make decisions that would lead them in the right direction. If your life is a trail of not-too-brilliant choices, own it. You don't make better decisions tomorrow by passing off yesterday's bad decisions as divine guidance.

An end in itself: On the one hand your story is important. On the other hand, God's story is the real story. We are mortal, he alone has immortality. We are finite, he is infinite. His story is before all stories. Our story begins and ends with his story. Because our story is a sub-set of his story, we are significant. Our story for its own sake is not that huge, but our significance lies in being part of his drama.

• Gather the checklists from each season and try to make a fair assessment of which seasons you have been through.

• What seasons do you think you have yet to experience?

• Do you have any sense of the timing of each season; how long might, say, a Skills Building Season take in your life?

• Are there some wrong decisions you need to correct before proceeding? What are you willing to do about them?

16.

I don't think I have the patience to create a tapestry—choosing just the right background color and fabric that will last for decades if not centuries; painstakingly creating an image for this blank piece of material; selecting the threads; deciding what to do first, what to do later; deliberating the richness of the image versus the time and skill it takes to weave the additional features; deciding on the fineness of the needlework; then hours of painstaking sewing, snipping, pushing and pulling. Just the thought of it overwhelms me.

Today we use computers to generate and transmit images, but the essence of creating the image is the same. We use words like granularity of the pixels or the dpi that parallel the world of tapestry and needlepoint... and painting by numbers. The blank screen, the image we want to create, the components of the picture. Before there were scanners, I sat, much like my mother at her cross-stitch, and clicked pixel by pixel to create crude black and white images.

What we have explored in this book can be related to your development of a life-tapestry in at least three ways:

1. Each person is unique, created with the potential to bear God's image. Each life is the material that forms the perfect background for the special tapestry God wants to create.

developing your tapestry

2. God has a blueprint for our lives. It may seem too broad and general to be of any real use: "To be conformed to the image of his own dear Son." Yet hovering above the fabric of our lives is the vision for who we can be by God's grace. It is a dream, a picture, a hope that will transform us. The sooner and the more completely we wrap our hearts and minds around the lines of God's blueprint, the better.

3. On top of the background of man's potential and the seemingly faint layer of God's plans "to give us a future and a hope" comes each person's picture, the real stuff of life. In the thoughtfulness and thoroughness and thickness of the threads we see our life choices laid plain. In one beautiful detail of our tapestry we see our obedience in following the Plan. In a corner a rusty needle dangles haplessly at the end of the dusty thread of neglect, brokenness or pain. In other spots we have woven "outside the lines" and it may look artistic, but it somehow doesn't flow with the rest of the picture. Some of our tapestries are rich with the blend of the Seven Seasons of life. Others are more color-scarce. Many of us have spent years creating tapestries that compartmentalize the major spheres of our lives. We walk through small gates between Career, Community, Call and Creativity, keeping them ever separate. Yet we admire those boundaryless tapestries where the everyday and the eternal flow easily together...where the majestic touches the mundane and transforms it.

WHY CREATE A TAPESTRY?

You and I each have a unique tapestry. Understanding our past can help us to more fully experience the future. As we move to greater understanding of our own journey towards Convergence, there are two equal and opposite errors:

- taking such pride in our past that it blinds us to a different future, and

- having such a poor understanding of our past that we waste decades reinventing ourselves only to find that we have "created" a new us that looks like many of our ancestors.

God is indeed the God of new beginnings. Many of us are grateful for new beginnings and are happy to forget a few chapters from our past. Clinging relentlessly to family ties and history can indeed impede personal growth. Yet our family history does impact us, and having some understanding of our roots can sometimes help us fashion a future that is deliberately different from—or that draws purposefully on—that past.

We have tried to convey the importance of understanding the story of our own tapestry. It can be an anchor that keeps us from being swept into despair, losing perspective, repeating poor family patterns and worse.

IN THE GENES

I have only recently discovered some things about my past. One Friday evening I read my grandfather's unpublished memoirs. Joseph Lewis Green had trained for the ministry after a start in the London business world as a teenager where he worked at the leading edge of the communications industry. (He sold Waterman fountain pens across the counter.) Some years later he was the minister of a church in the East End of London.

> The activities of the various organizations were seriously restricted by the limited accommodation. We resolved to build a two storey institute at a cost of four thousand pounds which was a considerable sum for those days and an heroic venture for a working class congregation, most of whom were artisans, factory workers and clerks.

Later he went on to write:

> The stone laying ceremony of the Institute was performed by Sir Frank Dyson, Astronomer Royal, who was the son of a Baptist minister. In spite of his eminence, Sir Frank was the soul of modesty... Sir George Hume, the Member of Parliament for Greenwich, also participated in the service... In three and a half years nearly the whole deficit was liquidated.

Around 60 years later I found myself in a very different business community, Silicon Valley. When I sensed God was leading me to start The

Institute, little did I know that J.L. Green had faced the same challenge; had I read his story a few years earlier, I would have been less surprised when I sensed God say, "Are you willing to start an institute?"

David Boyd has a clear illustration of this in his own story. In his own words,

> Consideration of being Chancellor of a university never appeared on the screen of my consciousness for the first forty-four years of my life. Then an opportunity came to serve through this role in 1992 with the University of the Nations/Kona. A few years later I discovered something while reviewing the history of our family name and lineage in Scotland. A number of the forebearers of the Boyd name were found in similar roles in fields of education, missions and government. They even included one Robert Boyd (1578-1627) who held the Chancellor role in Glasgow University in 1615 and at the University of Edinburgh in 1622.

What is there in your own story that suggests what God may or may not have for you?

THE CORE OF OUR IDENTITY

I closely examined a wheel from a Model-T Ford that was propped against a wall in an antique store. It had an old rubber tire, 12 sturdy wooden spokes, and a metal hub. I said to Lyn, "If it had ten spokes I would buy it." In an earlier chapter we introduced you to the 10-F Model. Think of each F as a spoke in a wheel. Each is needed for our completeness. At any point in time it seems as though repair or restoration is taking place on different spokes.

The hub is another key piece that keeps the wheel functioning. It represents our identity. We cannot easily come to Convergence without settling core identity issues. A good friend, Dr. Art Wouters has written a ThoughtPiece[64] in which he describes the seven things that lie at the center of our being. Think of his "seven hidden Ps" as seven ball bearings that are hidden, but enable the wheel to turn smoothly. Wouters' seven Ps are as follows:

---

[64] Dr. Art Wouters *The Hub*, © I* International, 1999. See ThoughtPieces at www.convergencebook.com

- **Presence:** The first is the longing for the presence and availability of at least one other person who will always be there for us and who will desire a relationship with us no matter what happens or whatever we do.

- **Provision:** The second is the longing for provision. My relational nature makes me dependent on others to provide for me, and others need me to help provide for them.

- **Protection:** The third longing is to be adequately protected and to be able to protect those who need it.

- **Permission:** The fourth longing is to be allowed to be ourselves. This is the most vital of all permissions needed from others.

- **Purity:** The fifth longing for relationship is one of a desire for purity. Ever since Adam and Eve sewed fig leaves to cover their nakedness, humans have needed to know how to deal with their moral guilt and shame.

- **Power:** The sixth longing of relationships concerns the dimension of power and control. Each individual is born for a purpose and with the capacity to make an impact on his or her world. To us has been given the authority to make an impact and we are all gifted in various ways to engage in personally and corporately fulfilling activities. Everyone needs to discover their Call and serve others and society in a responsible way. We can control some things and must learn to live with things that are not under our control. Many individuals either underestimate or overestimate their own power as a result of early defining disappointments. Whether you expect too much or too little from yourself, both options lead to a person failing to fulfill his or her potential.

- **Partnership:** The seventh longing of relationships is expressed in the desire for meaningful partnerships. We need others to partner with us in the completion of meaningful activities and we long for genuine partnership with others.

Settling central identity issues can be a major help towards Convergence.

Consider the tapestry of life: where might it have been woven different-ly if we were at rest with the seven hub/identity areas? Where would we have lived more, compensated less, given more freely...? Until we settle our identity in our Creator, until we pattern our tapestry after him, we will be so busy "making something of ourselves" that we will probably fail to even see his design. Until we know God as our provision, our pro-tection, and our purity; until we rest in his presence, his power (made perfect in our weakness); until we know his Yes, his permission; until we take his yoke, his partnership...until then, Convergence will be hard to come by. Why? Because when we "do our own thing" we sub-optimize. Because our tendency is towards disintegration, not integration. Because left to ourselves, we don't get it together.

A healthy hub comes in part from a fresh resting in this principle: "Lose your life, and you will find it." How smoothly does your wheel run?

CONSIDERED LIVING

By all accounts we should be a generation that has the freedom to pur-sue our dreams. Dishwashers, microwave ovens, vacuum cleaners, refrig-erators, cell phones, fax, e-mail, PDAs, pagers... We have more "moth-er's little helpers" than any other generation. We should have more free time than we do. In 1890 people were asked to list the items they con-sidered essential to everyday life. They listed 16 items. In 1995 the list had grown to 89 items. When we don't have a clear purpose, the clutter of modern life will flood into the vacuum. One of the issues here is that these "assistants" fill up our hands and our heads, but do little for our hearts.

Oftentimes we seem to be caught in a cycle of mechanical responses to the unending stream of information that the machine of life spews at us. Waist-deep in information, we plod pedestrianly around the corners of the information maze that leads who-knows-where. Patterned reactions to the routine transactions of daily life on planet earth. Random decisions aimed to cope, or at best to add some variety to our lives. These symp-toms seem to be life in its normative form. But this treadmill existence is not considered living.

The road to Convergence demands time to reflect. It requires pausing to consider the end[65], resting to make inner mid-course corrections[66], journaling to live twice, re-tracing ones steps. It means saying No to the conforming, selecting carefully from the basket of threads offered to us each day, picking out the permanent from the transient, the substantive from the superfluous, the precious from the precarious. Convergence means making the choices that favor the long-term dreams you whispered to your heart when away from the crowd. Convergence comes by making room for God, by having margin. This is closer to considered living.

Only God knows everything, and I suspect he resists man's attempts to create simple formulae for life. But this does not mean that we cannot seek to live deliberately. And if we want to live deliberately, it helps to be people of context. We find part of our context in what scripture says about our identity in Christ. The foundation of our identity and security is the sure love of Jesus. We find another part of our identity in the tapestry he has woven around us.

REVIEWING THE RAW MATERIALS FOR YOUR TAPESTRY

The fabric of your life

Certain things about you constitute the "fabric" of your life. Even before a design is sketched on that fabric, even before the first threads are woven, there is you. What are the things that make up your fabric? In earlier chapters we touched on how you are woven. Where are you different? What makes you unique? How do you carry in your fabric the weave of the family?

The Seasons

Taking the tapestry image further, the threads in your life are the Seven Seasons. They are like seven different colors woven in and out, back and forth, making the image of your life.

Which of the Seasons have you been through? What Season are you in right now? Does any pattern form in your mind as you consider the coming and going of seasons?

In my own life, the preparation seemed to take forever. Not that I did not love and pour myself into what I was doing at the time. But when Lyn and I were leading a youth group or pastoring a church, it felt like preparation, not destiny. And when I studied for about five years, this too felt like something I

---

[65] Psalm 73:16, 17
[66] Mark 6:31. "Come aside to a deserted place and rest awhile." And 1 Kings 17:2,3 "Then the word of the Lord came to him saying, 'Get away from here and turn eastward and hide by the brook Cherith, which flows into the Jordan.'"

had to do to get a ticket to the work life. Academia was not my destiny. And even though I worked in some companies for fourteen years and others for three, in all those years I felt like I was living in a tent. I felt a sense of caution about trying to make any of them my long-term home. They were Seasons of Skills Building, Internal Integrity testing, Gift discovery and development, Fearing and Hearing God....

Too often I have seen people trying to build a permanent home where God would have them pitch a tent. I see people trying desperately to make a career in a particular company when all of the indications are that they should be moving on. We need to be better attuned to why we are where we are at any point in time.

The opposite error is the career-hopping scenario where we do not stay long enough in any one place for God to get his work done in us. We assume that difficulty means that there is something wrong with our employer. In today's world of "Internet years" that are shorter than "dog years", how will we experience the character building that is an essential prerequisite to Convergence?

The Silver Threads

Woven through those seven different colors are the clear Sovereign touches on your tapestry. It is as if God himself has periodically taken a needle and woven a splash of silver, a touch of gold into your tapestry. These have become points of light that you look back to often. When you are losing perspective, you step back from the daily weave and remind yourself of these points of light.

For some the silver threads come as life experiences, for others they are the written word. Or it might be a prayer someone prays for you or an insight a complete stranger has into your life. Sometimes it is the quiet whisper of assurance in the morning after worrying in the night. Your life has those threads. Step back and see the silver.

Your Career, Creativity, Community

So you have the fabric of your life, and you have experienced many seasons. But how does it form an image? The answer is simple: one stitch at a time. Which raises the question: "how do I know that the stitches are all working together?" At the level of our humanness, we can have goals, objectives, life mission statements and more. Then hope for the best.

At another level, it is about obedience and who is going to be at the controls. It is that simple: will we trust God, or do we think we can do a better job.

As you look back on the Career/Community choices you have made, which ones would you like to change? How about Career/Creativity: are there choices you have made that have sacrificed your creative side for the sake of "getting ahead" in your career?

And what about the good choices you have made? What can you learn from them that can help you in the future?

Your Call

Call. Even the word sounds like an outside-in sort of thing; something that happens to us, something we have to wait for. And this is true. But it is also true that "deep calls to deep." The external call is to the internal "us" as human beings, not as automatons. The call we receive is consistent with our story, with our fabric, and more important, with the "image of God" that is imprinted on the fabric of our lives. It is colored by our seasons, and touched with the silver threads of God's sovereignty.

Because "Call" can be hard to define for some folk, we like to ask people about their passion. We ask the question in as many ways as we can. What rings your bell? What gets you up in the morning? What do you care deeply about? What lights your fuse? What gets your motor running? What gives you deep pleasure? When do you feel most at peace? About what do you say, "I could do this for a long time"?

If our Call is not clear, it can sometimes be because we are not ready to hear it.

STATE OF READINESS

When we are willing to do God's will, we are ready to hear it. There is good reason why the sun rises and sets in a cycle, why we eat three or so meals a day and sleep each night. There is a renewing possibility in daily life. Each day brings opportunity, but also the temptation to take an easy way out. Forget all this weaving; pass the spray paint! Forget the deliberate discovery of our God and his ways, let me just scan an image from a famous media, business or sports personality so I can be like him or her... and if he or she wears a cross, so much the easier. But being molded in the image of someone else—even an unrealistic image we have of ourselves—is a dead-end street.

Our readiness to obey needs daily renewing. If we are to avoid becoming crusty cynics or heartless theoreticians, we need to constantly re-assess our own state of readiness. If we are to avoid the discontentment that comes from fashioning ourselves after the successful, we must obey God not so that we too can be successful, but so that we can walk out our Call. This requires a continual state of readiness.

• How ready are we to choose the seasons?
• Are we willing to forego the shortcuts?
• Do we have a desire to have our minds renewed? Are we open to imagining our identity and our actions being in alignment with God?
• Are we ready to daily commit to integration?

These and other questions are explored in the Convergence Readiness Assessment exercise at www.convergencebook.com.

ONE SIZE...

There is no "one size fits all" prescription to the journey towards Convergence. In fact, there is no prescription at all. There are principles that when wisely applied can make you better equipped to sift through the confusing options that we encounter. We have attempted to provide meaningful handles for life through the concepts of finding the overlaps between the Four Cs of Career, Creativity, Community and Call and the embracing of the kairos seasons of life.

In an earlier chapter we described Convergence this way:

The Process of Convergence:
The coming together of those important deposits that have been built into your life over the past 40-or-so years that result in you discovering and walking in your life Call.

The Activities of Convergence:
Cooperating in understanding, preparing for, and walking into your Creator's life purposes for you.

The End of Convergence:
The discovery of those threads which when woven together at a particular juncture in your life, cause you to say "Yes!, This is me; this is what my life is for."

Convergence is not necessarily about setting out to do great things. Convergence comes through setting one's face towards a walk of obedience that is carried to completion. In this book we hope to direct four separated areas of life—Career, Community, Creativity, and Call—towards a common center.

The world around us is changing rapidly and radically. The only sure way to navigate the change we are encountering is rapid and radical obedience. People intuitively hunger for an integrated life. They hunger for a world where family does not have to be sacrificed on the altar of work, where creativity does not have to be neutered, where the deep call within finds expression without. And when they see it in you, they will believe it. Our challenge to you is simple: take up the road towards Convergence. Abandon the shortcuts of orderliness and balance, and pursue obedience. Life is a life of faith: make sure your faith is in God. Deliberately move away from that which provides the escape of faith in a company, a church, a career-path, a stock market or your own smarts. They will not be enough. Submit yourself to the ways in which God disciplines you. Embrace the Seasons; grow in character. Make the small daily choices of obedience so that you learn the ways of God. Then when the big decisions come, you will be prepared for them.

God paid a high price for reconciliation. That reconciliation extends beyond our so-called spiritual lives. "For God was in Christ reconciling *all things* to himself..." Our challenge to you: lay yourself on this template of truth so that all things in your life will indeed be reconciled, aligned, integrated with God, through his Son Jesus Christ.

> There remains therefore a Sabbath rest for the people of God. For the one who has entered his rest has himself rested from his own works... let us therefore be diligent to enter that rest... Hebrews 4:9-11.

17.

By Vaughan Granier

I arrived in Heaven and stood in line to face the Lord. Other people carried beautifully wrapped gifts and, holding them carefully to prevent damage, stood ready for their name to be called.

I looked at my empty hands. Why didn't I have a gift? Everyone else seemed to. Yet, it wasn't as if they had collected their gifts from somewhere else and arrived with them; the gifts seemed to be part of them.

To try and understand what was different about me, I asked a few people about their gifts. But the answers were all the same. "I'm sorry. I don't know about you. My gift is the work I have accomplished for my Lord. These are the projects I did, the plans I had for my life that I brought to fruition as a Christian. This is what I am offering to the Lord. I have waited my whole life for this. I don't understand why you don't have such a gift for the Lord."

I became insecure and feared the Judgment of the Lord. I could only imagine standing giftless before the Throne of Grace and being singled out by the Lord as the only one not bearing a gift.

Before I knew it, my name was called, and I walked slowly towards the Throne of the Lord. It was not that I feared Him, but I was imagining stepping up to the Judgment seat and saying to

God, "I am sorry—all these others have brought you gifts, big and small, and there has been such ceremony each time. Their life's work is before you and you have been pleased with it. I have no such gift to offer you. I do not have a significant thing that I have achieved which consumed my whole life."

The Lord rose from His seat, smiled and said, "Do not trouble yourself about offering me a gift today. Come with me—I have something to show you. I've been waiting, looking forward to the time when you would come before me. Every day that you walked with me I received something from you and I have kept these things to show you."

He took me to a room, the four walls of which contained a magnificent tapestry of familiar scenes and details from my life. But it wasn't so much my life being illustrated as the times when the lives of others and the Kingdom of God touched mine. At every point where my life touched someone else's, there began two golden threads—the one leading from my life into theirs, and the other leading from their life into mine. God looked at this Tapestry with deep affection and traced with His finger along each golden thread from start to finish.

As I watched and looked at the expression on His face, I began to see the effect of the golden threads on the tapestry. They brightened certain sections that otherwise would have been very dark. They drew together two, sometimes more, sections with a complexity and intricacy of design that left me astounded. In certain places they formed a basket, of sorts, a support-type structure that framed and held a scene from another's life. Sometimes the threads seemed to form a path between areas of the tapestry—a path that enabled a flow and a progression from one scene to another with no chance of going astray.

After a long while, the Lord turned to me and said, "Do you see? Each golden thread is your act of obedience. Sometimes you obeyed my urging to act, to speak into or to intercede for another's life. Other times, because you tuned your ear to hear my voice, you heard and did what I asked. Sometimes you chose to hear the voices of others and, in humility, allowed my Spirit to change you.

These golden threads of obedience were your gift to me every day of your life; this tapestry is the sum total of those gifts. You do not stand before me empty handed, my little one. You stand before me obedient, day-by-day, opportunity-by-opportunity, and your gift of obedience is so huge that you could not have carried it into my presence, even if you had been aware of what it was. It is also more complicated and intricate than human hands could have woven. The beauty of a life poured out as a daily offering, and the beauty of a love expressed through the obedience that is detailed and remembered for all time before us here could not have been crafted by human hands.

This work, I kept for My angels to do. This tapestry has been woven joyfully in secret by my angels who have watched and celebrated your life and your obedience to me. This has been a lifetime's work—your lifetime, their joyful work. They stand in this audience behind you, honored to have woven this for you. You sent them such volumes and quality of material, that their work was easy. This tapestry has been made for this day, this time, and this place. It is revealed now, to be your gift to me."

Somehow, in listening to Him, I had not seen the room change. While the tapestry remained, there were no longer walls. We were again before the Throne of Grace, and the words he spoke were no longer a gentle conversation—they were his Judgment over my life. As with each life that had gone before me, Heaven broke into thunderous applause at the Judgment, and as I walked away from the Throne to the place reserved for me, I began to realize that my steps were taking me into a gallery of people who were familiar beyond all expectation. I saw reflected in their faces the golden threads that I had sewn in their life, and the threads that they had sewn in mine.

These people were my inheritance. The tapestry was my gift.